The Liturgical Psalter and Canticles

The Liturgical Psalter and Canticles

As used in

An Australian Prayer Book

The Alternative Service Book 1980

Alternative Prayer Book 1984
Church of Ireland

Set to Anglican Chants

for use on Sundays, Festivals,
Holy Days and Various Occasions
in ASB Tables

Edited by Lionel Dakers
and Cyril Taylor

Collins

The Editors

Dr Lionel Dakers is Director of the Royal School of Church Music.

Canon Cyril Taylor is a Director of *Hymns Ancient and Modern*. He has served on the Liturgical Commission and was for some years a member of the Religious Broadcasting Department of the BBC.

Collins Liturgical Publications
187 Piccadilly, London W1V 9DA

ISBN 0 00 599680 5
First published 1981
Fourth printing 1984

Music setting by MSS Studios and typesetting by Ferndown Typesetters, 19 Stour Road, Christchurch, Dorset.
Printed in Great Britain by Hazell Watson & Viney Limited, Member of the BPCC Group, Aylesbury, Bucks

INDEX OF CANTICLES

INDEX OF CHANTS

INDEX OF CHANTS

INDEX OF CHANTS

PREFACE

As its title implies, this book is for choirs in churches which use *The Alternative Service Book 1980*. It includes all the Canticles provided there for use at Morning and Evening Prayer, together with all those Psalms—but only those—selected for use, in whole or in part, in Tables 1 and 3.

Compared with the size of page used in the original Collins edition of *The Psalms, a new translation for worship,* and still more markedly, in the ASB, the page size of this present edition is much larger. This means that the lines can be longer and that the sign ⌣, used to indicate a 'carry-over' from one line to the next, can here be dispensed with altogether.

The following rules must apply for the chanting:

1 Always take a breath at an asterisk.

2 Where there is an extra space between words, make a break (a 'mental comma'), but without taking a breath.

3 When there are more than two syllables within a bar · the centred dot shows how they should be divided.

4 The sign † shows that the second half of a double chant should be used.

5 The final '-ed' should not be pronounced as a separate syllable unless it carries an accent (e.g. blessèd).

The following should also be noted:

a Verses within square brackets may be omitted.

b The Jewish doxologies which conclude Psalms 41, 72, and 106 are printed in brackets. If the usual Christian doxology ('Glory to the Father . . . ') is sung, these may be omitted.

c The *Gloria* will be found at the end of every Canticle which requires it. If it is not printed with a Canticle, it is not to be sung.

The Music

1 When a Psalm or Canticle is likely to be often used, a choice of chants is given for use in rotation.

2 Certain chants appear in a lower key than usual. This is to avoid unduly high reciting notes.

3 Passing notes have been omitted, unless the character of the chant was thought to be impaired by such omission.

The Editors are grateful to Michael Fleming for his advice on the choice of chants.

THE CANTICLES
MORNING

Venite

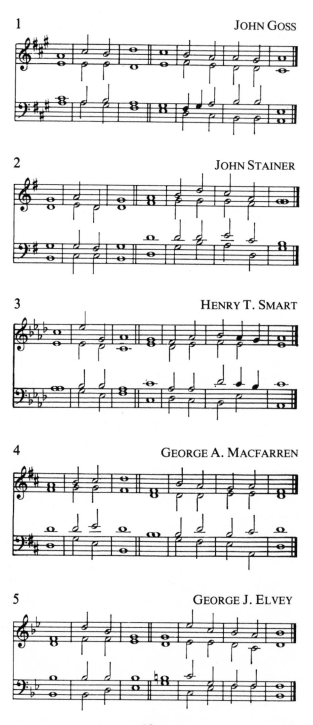

1   JOHN GOSS

2   JOHN STAINER

3   HENRY T. SMART

4   GEORGE A. MACFARREN

5   GEORGE J. ELVEY

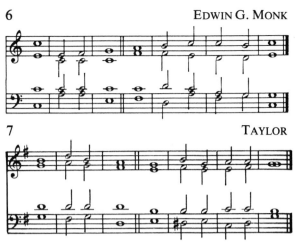

6   EDWIN G. MONK

7   TAYLOR

8   GEORGE C. MARTIN

1 O come let us sing ˈ out · to the ˈ Lord:
    let us shout in triumph to the ˈ rock of ˈ our salˈvation.

2 Let us come before his ˈ face with ˈ thanksgiving:
    and cry ˈ out to · him ˈ joyfully · in ˈ psalms.

3 For the Lord is a ˈ great ˈ God:
    and a great ˈ king a·bove ˈ all ˈ gods.

4 In his hand are the ˈ depths · of the ˈ earth:
    and the peaks of the ˈ mountains · are ˈ his ˈ also.

† 5 The sea is his and ˈ he ˈ made it:
    his hands ˈ moulded ˈ dry ˈ land.

6 Come let us worship and ˈ bow ˈ down:
    and kneel beˈfore the ˈ Lord our ˈ maker.

7 For he is the ˈ Lord our ˈ God:
    we are his ˈ people · and the ˈ sheep of · his ˈ pasture.

8 If only you would hear his ˈ voice toˈday:
    for he ˈ comes to ˈ judge the ˈ earth.

9 He shall judge the ˈ world with ˈ righteousness:
    and the ˈ peoples ˈ with his ˈ truth.

Glory to the Father and ˈ to the ˈ Son:
    and ˈ to the ˈ Holy ˈ Spirit;
as it was in the beˈginning is ˈ now:
    and shall be for ˈ ever. ˈ Aˈmen.

Jubilate

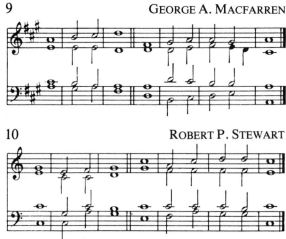

9   GEORGE A. MACFARREN

10   ROBERT P. STEWART

11   THOMAS NORRIS

12   IVOR ATKINS

1   O shout to the Lord in triumph ˈ all the ˈ earth:
    serve the Lord with gladness * and come before his ˈ face with ˈ songs of ˈ joy.

2   Know that the Lord ˈ he is ˈ God:
    it is he who has made us and we are his *
     we are his ˈ people · and the ˈ sheep of · his ˈ pasture.

3   Come into his gates with thanksgiving * and into his ˈ courts with ˈ praise:
    give thanks to him and ˈ bless his ˈ holy ˈ name.

4   For the Lord is good * his loving mercy ˈ is for ˈ ever:
    his faithfulness throughˈout all ˈ generˈations.

    Glory to the Father and ˈ to the ˈ Son:
     and ˈ to the ˈ Holy ˈ Spirit;
   as it was in the beˈginning is ˈ now:
     and shall be for ˈ ever. ˈ Aˈmen.

The Easter Anthems

HENRY T. SMART

13

HENRY G. LEY

14

JOSEPH BARNBY

15

1 Christ our passover has been ˈ sacri·ficed ˈ for us:
    so let us ˈ celeˈbrate the ˈ feast,

2 not with the old leaven of corˈruption · and ˈ wickedness:
    but with the unleavened ˈ bread of · sinˈcerity · and ˈ truth.

3 Christ once raised from the dead ˈ dies no ˈ more:
    death has no ˈ more doˈminion ˈ over him.

4 In dying he died to sin ˈ once for ˈ all:
    in ˈ living · he ˈ lives to ˈ God.

5 See yourselves therefore as ˈ dead to ˈ sin:
    and alive to God in ˈ Jesus ˈ Christ our ˈ Lord.

6 Christ has been ˈ raised · from the ˈ dead:
    the ˈ firstfruits · of ˈ those who ˈ sleep.

7 For as by ˈ man came ˈ death:
    by man has come also the resurˈrection ˈ of the ˈ dead;

8 for as in ˈ Adam · all ˈ die:
    even so in Christ shall ˈ all be ˈ made aˈlive.

Glory to the Father and ˈ to the ˈ Son:
    and ˈ to the ˈ Holy ˈ Spirit;
as it was in the beˈginning is ˈ now:
    and shall be for ˈ ever. ˈ Aˈmen.

Another chant overleaf

16

GEORGE THALBEN-BALL

1 Christ our passover has been | sacri·ficed | for us:
so let us | cele|brate the | feast,

2 not with the old leaven of cor|ruption · and | wickedness:
but with the unleavened | bread of · sin|cerity · and | truth.

3 Christ once raised from the dead | dies no | more:
death has no | more do|minion | over him.

4 In dying he died to sin | once for | all:
in | living · he | lives to | God.

5 See yourselves therefore as | dead to | sin:
and alive to God in | Jesus | Christ our | Lord.

6 Christ has been | raised · from the | dead:
the | firstfruits · of | those who | sleep.

7 For as by | man came | death:
by man has come also the resur|rection | of the | dead;

8 for as in | Adam · all | die:
even so in Christ shall | all be | made a|live.

Glory to the Father and | to the | Son:
and | to the | Holy | Spirit;
as it was in the be|ginning is | now:
and shall be for | ever. | A|men.

Benedictus
(The Song of Zechariah)

17

JOHN LEMON

18

HIGHMORE SKEATS Junior

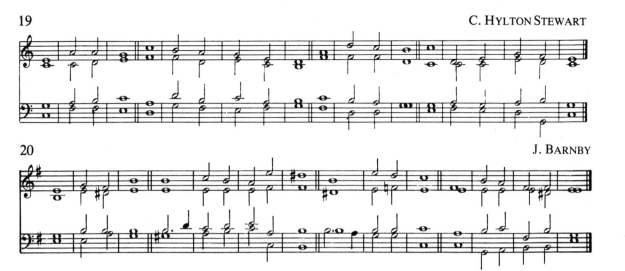

19 C. HYLTON STEWART

20 J. BARNBY

1 Blessèd be the Lord the | God of | Israel:
   for he has come to his | people · and | set them | free.

2 He has raised up for us a | mighty | saviour:
   born of the | house · of his | servant | David.

3 Through his holy prophets he | promised · of | old:
   that he would save us from our enemies * from the | hands of | all that | hate us.

4 He promised to show | mercy · to our | fathers:
   and to re|member · his | holy | covenant.

5 This was the oath he swore to our | father | Abraham:
   to set us | free · from the | hands of · our | enemies,

6 free to worship him with|out | fear:
   holy and righteous in his sight | all the | days of · our | life.

7 You my child shall be called the prophet of the | Most | High:
   for you will go before the | Lord · to pre|pare his | way,

8 to give his people knowledge | of sal|vation:
   by the for|giveness · of | all their | sins.

9 In the tender compassion | of our | God:
   the dawn from on | high shall | break up|on us,

10 to shine on those who dwell in darkness and the | shadow · of | death:
   and to guide our feet | into · the | way of | peace.

   Glory to the Father and | to the | Son:
   and | to the | Holy | Spirit;
   as it was in the be|ginning is | now:
   and shall be for | ever. | A|men.

15

A Song of Creation

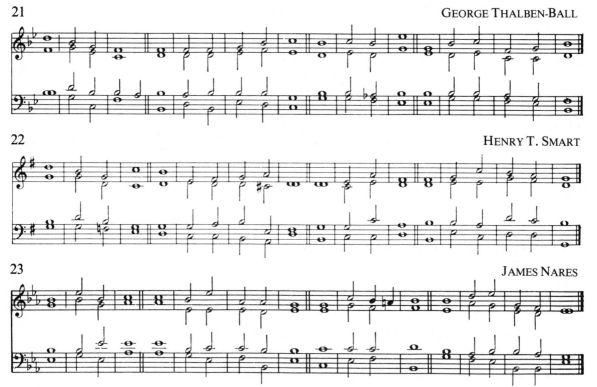

21   GEORGE THALBEN-BALL

22   HENRY T. SMART

23   JAMES NARES

For a short version, verses 4-17 may be omitted

1   Bless the Lord all cre|ated | things:
      sing his | praise · and ex|alt him · for | ever.

2   Bless the | Lord you | heavens:
      sing his | praise · and ex|alt him · for | ever.

3   Bless the Lord you | angels · of the | Lord:
      bless the | Lord all | you his | hosts;

4   bless the Lord you waters a|bove the | heavens:
      sing his | praise · and ex|alt him · for | ever.

5   Bless the Lord | sun and | moon:
      bless the | Lord you | stars of | heaven;

6   bless the Lord all | rain and | dew:
      sing his | praise · and ex|alt him · for | ever.

7   Bless the Lord all | winds that | blow:
      bless the | Lord you | fire and | heat;

8   bless the Lord scorching wind and | bitter | cold:
      sing his | praise · and ex|alt him · for | ever.

9   Bless the Lord dews and | falling | snows:
      bless the | Lord you | nights and | days;

10 bless the Lord ' light and ' darkness:
   sing his ' praise · and ex'alt him · for ' ever.

11 Bless the Lord ' frost and ' cold:
   bless the ' Lord you ' ice and ' snow;

12 bless the Lord ' lightnings · and ' clouds:
   sing his ' praise · and ex'alt him · for ' ever.

13 O let the earth ' bless the ' Lord:
   bless the ' Lord you ' mountains · and ' hills;

14 bless the Lord all that ' grows · in the ' ground:
   sing his ' praise · and ex'alt him · for ' ever.

15 Bless the ' Lord you ' springs:
   bless the ' Lord you ' seas and ' rivers;

16 bless the Lord you whales and all that ' swim · in the ' waters:
   sing his ' praise · and ex'alt him · for ' ever.

17 Bless the Lord all ' birds · of the ' air:
   bless the ' Lord you ' beasts and ' cattle;

18 bless the Lord all ' men · on the ' earth:
   sing his ' praise · and ex'alt him · for ' ever.

19 O People of God ' bless the ' Lord:
   bless the ' Lord you ' priests · of the ' Lord;

20 bless the Lord you ' servants · of the ' Lord:
   sing his ' praise · and ex'alt him · for ' ever.

21 Bless the Lord all men of ' upright ' spirit:
   bless the Lord you that are ' holy · and ' humble · in ' heart.

   Bless the Father the Son and the ' Holy ' Spirit:
   sing his ' praise · and ex'alt him · for ever.

Great and Wonderful

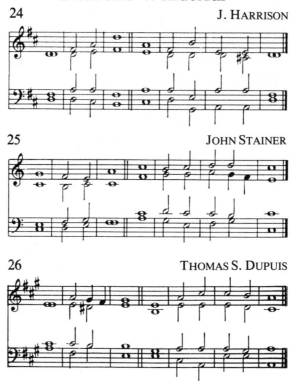

24   J. HARRISON

25   JOHN STAINER

26   THOMAS S. DUPUIS

1   Great and wonderful are your deeds Lord ˈ God · the Alˈmighty:
   just and true are your ˈ ways O ˈ King · of the ˈ nations.

2   Who shall not revere and praise your ˈ name O ˈ Lord?
   for ˈ you aˈlone are ˈ holy.

3   All nations shall come and worship ˈ in your ˈ presence:
   for your just ˈ dealings · have ˈ been reˈvealed.

    To him who sits on the throne ˈ and · to the ˈ Lamb:
   be praise and honour glory and might * for ever and ˈ ever. ˈ Aˈmen.

Te Deum

27: SET A   'TRENT'

28: SET B
EDWARD J. HOPKINS

29: SET C
JOHN DAVY

30: SET D
CHARLES V. STANFORD

1 You are ˈ God · and we ˈ praise you:
    you are the ˈ Lord and ˈ we acˈclaim you;

2 you are the eˈternal ˈ Father:
    all creˈation ˈ worships ˈ you.

3 To you all angels * all the ˈ powers of ˈ heaven:
    cherubim and seraphim ˈ sing in ˈ endless ˈ praise,

4 Holy holy holy Lord * God of ˈ power and ˈ might:
    heaven and ˈ earth are ˈ full of · your ˈ glory.

5 The glorious company of apˈostles ˈ praise you:
    the noble fellowship of prophets praise you *
        the white-robed ˈ army · of ˈ martyrs ˈ praise you.

6 Throughout the world the holy ˈ Church acˈclaims you:
    Father of ˈ majesˈty unˈbounded;

† 7 your true and only Son * worthy of ˈ all ˈ worship;
    and the Holy ˈ Spirit ˈ advocate · and ˈ guide.

continued

31: SET A   WILLIAM HAWES

32: SET B   JOHN L. HOPKINS

33: SET C   ROBERT COOKE

34: SET D   CHARLES V. STANFORD

8   You Christ are the ˈ King of ˈ glory:
    the eˈternal ˈ Son · of the ˈ Father.

9   When you became man to ˈ set us ˈ free:
    you did not abˈhor the ˈ Virgin's ˈ womb.

10 You overcame the ˈ sting of ˈ death:
    and opened the kingdom of ˈ heaven · to ˈ all beˈlievers.

11 You are seated at God's right ˈ hand in ˈ glory:
    we believe that you will ˈ come and ˈ be our ˈ judge.

12 Come then Lord and ˈ help your ˈ people:
    bought with the ˈ price of ˈ your own ˈ blood;

13 and bring us ˈ with your ˈ saints:
    to ˈ glory ˈ everˈlasting.

35: SET A

HENRY ALDRICH

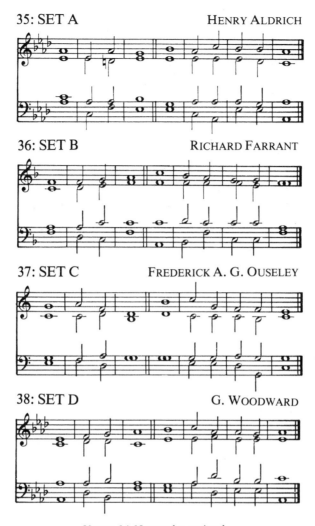

36: SET B

RICHARD FARRANT

37: SET C

FREDERICK A. G. OUSELEY

38: SET D

G. WOODWARD

Verses 14-18 may be omitted

14 Save your people Lord and | bless · your in|heritance:
    govern and up|hold them | now and | always.

15 Day by | day we | bless you:
    we | praise your | name for | ever.

16 Keep us today Lord from | all | sin:
    have mercy | on us | Lord have | mercy.

17 Lord show us your | love and | mercy;
    for we | put our | trust in | you.

18 In you Lord | is our | hope:
    let us not be con|founded | at the | last.

Gloria in Excelsis

39: SET A GEORGE A. MACFARREN

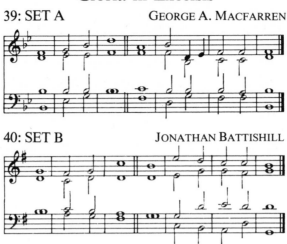

40: SET B JONATHAN BATTISHILL

1 Glory to | God · in the | highest:
   and | peace · to his | people · on | earth.

2 Lord God | heaven·ly | King:
   al|mighty | God and | Father,

3 we worship you we | give you | thanks:
   we | praise you | for your | glory.

41: SET A W. STERNDALE BENNETT

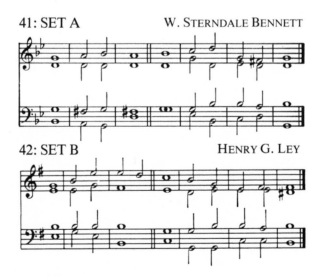

42: SET B HENRY G. LEY

4 Lord Jesus Christ only | Son · of the | Father:
   Lord | God | Lamb of | God,

5 you take away the | sin · of the | world:
   have | mercy | on | us;

6 you are seated at the right hand | of the | Father:
   re|ceive | our | prayer.

43: SET A

GEORGE A. MACFARREN

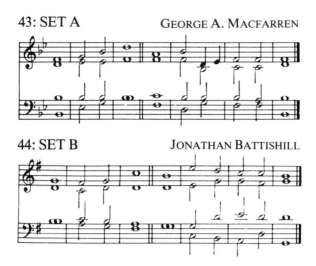

44: SET B

JONATHAN BATTISHILL

7 For you a⎸lone · are the ⎸Holy One:
   you a⎸lone ⎸ are the ⎸ Lord,

8 you alone are the Most High * Jesus Christ with the ⎸ Holy ⎸ Spirit:
   in the glory of God the ⎸ Father. ⎸ A⎸men.

Saviour of the World

45   ALAN GRAY

46   C. HUBERT H. PARRY

47   JOHN GOSS

1   Jesus saviour of the world * come to us | in your | mercy:
       we look to | you to | save and | help us.

2   By your cross and your life laid down * you set your | people | free:
       we look to | you to | save and | help us.

3   When they were ready to perish you | saved · your dis|ciples:
       we look to | you to | come to · our | help.

4   In the greatness of your mercy loose us | from our | chains:
       forgive the | sins of | all your | people.

5   Make yourself known as our saviour and | mighty · de|liverer:
       save and | help us · that | we may | praise you.

6   Come now and dwell with us | Lord Christ | Jesus:
       hear our | prayer · and be | with us | always.

† 7   And when you | come in · your | glory:
       make us to be one with you * and to | share the | life of · your | kingdom.

EVENING

Psalm 134

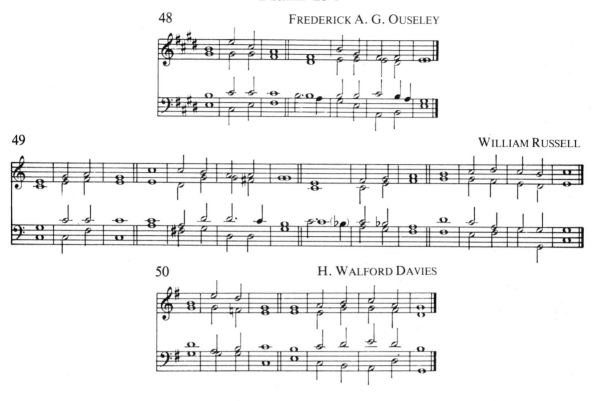

48   FREDERICK A. G. OUSELEY

49   WILLIAM RUSSELL

50   H. WALFORD DAVIES

1   Come bless the Lord   all you ⏐ servants · of the ⏐ Lord:
      you that by night ⏐ stand · in the ⏐ house of · our ⏐ God.

2   Lift up your hands toward the holy place and ⏐ bless the ⏐ Lord:
      may the Lord bless you from Zion *
        the ⏐ Lord who · made ⏐ heaven · and ⏐ earth.

Glory to the Father and ⏐ to the ⏐ Son:
    and ⏐ to the ⏐ Holy ⏐ Spirit;
as it was in the be⏐ginning is ⏐ now:
    and shall be for ⏐ ever. ⏐ A⏐men.

Magnificat
(The Song of Mary)

JAMES TURLE

51

WILLIAM KNYVETT (from Handel)

52

1 My soul proclaims the ˈ greatness · of the ˈ Lord:
    my spirit reˈjoices · in ˈ God my ˈ saviour;

2 for he has looked with favour on his ˈ lowly ˈ servant:
    from this day all generˈations · will ˈ call me ˈ blessèd;

† 3 the Almighty has done ˈ great things ˈ for me:
    and ˈ holy ˈ is his ˈ name.

4 He has mercy on ˈ those who ˈ fear him:
    in ˈ every ˈ generˈation.

5 He has shown the ˈ strength · of his ˈ arm:
    he has scattered the ˈ proud in ˈ their conˈceit.

6 He has cast down the mighty ˈ from their ˈ thrones:
    and has ˈ lifted ˈ up the ˈ lowly.

7 He has filled the hungry with ˈ good ˈ things:
    and the rich he has ˈ sent aˈway ˈ empty.

8 He has come to the help of his ˈ servant ˈ Israel:
    for he has reˈmembered · his ˈ promise · of ˈ mercy,

9 the promise he ˈ made · to our ˈ fathers:
    to Abraham ˈ and his ˈ children · forˈever.

Glory to the Father and ˈ to the ˈ Son:
    and ˈ to the ˈ Holy ˈ Spirit;
as it was in the beˈginning is ˈ now:
    and shall be for ˈ ever. ˈ Aˈmen.

53

54

1 My soul proclaims the ǀ greatness · of the ǀ Lord:
  my spirit reǀjoices · in ǀ God my ǀ saviour;

2 for he has looked with favour on his ǀ lowly ǀ servant:
  from this day all generǀations · will ǀ call me ǀ blessèd;

† 3 the Almighty has done ǀ great things ǀ for me:
  and ǀ holy ǀ is his ǀ name.

4 He has mercy on ǀ those who ǀ fear him:
  in ǀ every ǀ generǀation.

5 He has shown the ǀ strength · of his ǀ arm:
  he has scattered the ǀ proud in ǀ their conǀceit.

6 He has cast down the mighty ǀ from their ǀ thrones:
  and has ǀ lifted ǀ up the ǀ lowly.

7 He has filled the hungry with ǀ good ǀ things:
  and the rich he has ǀ sent aǀway ǀ empty.

8 He has come to the help of his ǀ servant ǀ Israel:
  for he has reǀmembered · his ǀ promise · of ǀ mercy,

9 the promise he ǀ made · to our ǀ fathers:
  to Abraham ǀ and his ǀ children · forǀever.

  Glory to the Father and ǀ to the ǀ Son:
  and ǀ to the ǀ Holy ǀ Spirit;
  as it was in the beǀginning is ǀ now:
  and shall be for ǀ ever. ǀ Aǀmen.

Bless the Lord

55   JAMES TURLE

56   J. NARES

57   JAMES TURLE

1   Bless the Lord the ˈ God of · our ˈ fathers:
     sing his ˈ praise · and exˈalt him · for ˈ ever.

2   Bless his holy and ˈ glori·ous ˈ name:
     sing his ˈ praise · and exˈalt him · for ˈ ever.

3   Bless him in his holy and ˈ glori·ous ˈ temple:
     sing his ˈ praise · and exˈalt him · for ˈ ever.

4   Bless him who beˈholds the ˈ depths:
     sing his ˈ praise · and exˈalt him · for ˈ ever.

5   Bless him who sits beˈtween the ˈ cherubim:
     sing his ˈ praise · and exˈalt him · for ˈ ever.

6   Bless him on the ˈ throne of · his ˈ kingdom:
     sing his ˈ praise · and exˈalt him · for ˈ ever.

7   Bless him in the ˈ heights of ˈ heaven:
     sing his ˈ praise · and exˈalt him · for ˈ ever.

    Bless the Father the Son and the ˈ Holy ˈ Spirit:
     sing his ˈ praise · and exˈalt him · for ˈ ever.

Nunc Dimittis

(The Song of Simeon)

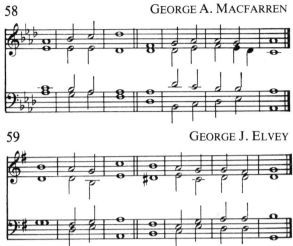

58 GEORGE A. MACFARREN

59 GEORGE J. ELVEY

60 GEORGE J. ELVEY

61 EDWIN G. MONK

1 Lord now you let your servant | go in | peace:
 your | word has | been ful|filled.

2 My own eyes have | seen the· sal|vation:
 which you have prepared in the | sight of | every | people;

† 3 a light to re|veal you · to the | nations:
 and the | glory · of your | people | Israel.

Glory to the Father and | to the | Son:
 and | to the | Holy | Spirit;
as it was in the be|ginning is | now:
 and shall be for | ever. | A|men.

29

The Song of Christ's Glory

62

J. STAFFORD SMITH

63

FREDERICK A. G. OUSELEY

1 Christ Jesus was in the ˈ form of ˈ God:
   but he did not ˈ cling · to eˈquality · with ˈ God.

2 He emptied himself * taking the ˈ form · of a ˈ servant:
   and was ˈ born · in the ˈ likeness · of ˈ men.

3 Being found in human form he ˈ humbled · himˈself:
   and became obedient unto death ˈ even ˈ death · on a ˈ cross.

4 Therefore God has ˈ highly · exˈalted him:
   and bestowed on him the ˈ name a·bove ˈ every ˈ name,

5 that at the name of Jesus every ˈ knee should ˈ bow:
   in heaven and on ˈ earth and ˈ under · the ˈ earth;

6 and every tongue confess that Jesus ˈ Christ is ˈ Lord:
   to the ˈ glory · of ˈ God the ˈ Father.

   Glory to the Father and ˈ to the ˈ Son:
      and ˈ to the ˈ Holy ˈ Spirit;
   as it was in the beˈginning is ˈ now:
      and shall be for ˈ ever. ˈ Aˈmen.

Glory and Honour

64   ANONYMOUS

65   JONATHAN BATTISHILL

1 Glory and ¦ honour · and ¦ power:
    are yours by ¦ right O ¦ Lord our ¦ God:

2 for you cre¦ated ¦ all things:
    and by your ¦ will they ¦ have their ¦ being.

3 Glory and ¦ honour · and ¦ power:
    are yours by ¦ right O ¦ Lamb · who was ¦ slain;

4 for by your blood you ransomed ¦ men for ¦ God:
    from every race and language * from ¦ every ¦ people · and ¦ nation,

5 to make them a ¦ kingdom · of ¦ priests:
    to stand and ¦ serve be¦fore our ¦ God.

    To him who sits on the throne ¦ and · to the ¦ Lamb:
    be praise and honour glory and might * for ever and ¦ ever. ¦ A¦men.

THE PSALMS

1

GEORGE J. ELVEY

1 Blessèd is the man who has not walked in the counsel ˈ of the · unˈgodly:
   nor followed the way of sinners * nor taken his ˈ seat aˈmongst the ˈ scornful.

2 But his delight is in the ˈ law · of the ˈ Lord:
   and on that law will he ˈ ponder ˈ day and ˈ night.

3 He is like a tree planted beside ˈ streams of ˈ water:
   that yields its ˈ fruit in ˈ due ˈ season.

4 Its leaves also ˈ shall not ˈ wither:
   and look   whatˈever · he ˈ does · it shall ˈ prosper.

5 As for the ungodly * it is not ˈ so with ˈ them:
   they are like the ˈ chaff · which the ˈ wind ˈ scatters.

6 Therefore the ungodly shall not stand ˈ up · at the ˈ judgement:
   nor sinners in the congreˈgation ˈ of the ˈ righteous.

† 7 For the Lord cares for the ˈ way · of the ˈ righteous:
   but the ˈ way of · the unˈgodly · shall ˈ perish.

2

ROBERT COOKE

1 Why are the | nations · in | tumult:
and why do the peoples | cherish · a |, vain | dream?

2 The kings of the earth rise up * and the rulers con|spire to|gether:
against the Lord and a|gainst · his an|ointed | saying,

† 3 'Let us break their | bonds a|sunder:
let us throw | off their | chains | from us.'

4 He that dwells in heaven shall | laugh them · to | scorn:
the Lord will | hold them | in de|rision.

5 Then will he speak to them in his wrath * and terrify them | in his | fury:
'I the Lord have set up my king on | Zion · my | holy | hill.'

6 I will announce the Lord's decree * that which | he has | spoken:
'You are my son   this | day have | I be|gotten you.

7 'Ask of me * and I will give you the nations for | your in|heritance:
the uttermost parts of the | earth for | your pos|session.

† 8 'You shall break them with a | rod of | iron:
and shatter them in | pieces · like a | potter's | vessel.'

9 Now therefore be | wise O | kings:
be advised   you that are | judges | of the | earth.

10 Serve the Lord with awe * and govern yourselves in | fear and | trembling:
lest he be angry and you | perish | in your | course.

† 11 For his wrath is | quickly | kindled:
blessèd are those that | turn to | him for | refuge.

3

EDWIN G. MONK

1 Lord how numerous ˈ are my ˈ enemies:
  many they ˈ are that ˈ rise aˈgainst me.

2 Many there are that ˈ talk of me · and ˈ say:
  'There is no ˈ help for · him ˈ in his ˈ God.'

3 But you Lord are about me ˈ as a ˈ shield:
  you are my glory   and the ˈ lifter ˈ up · of my ˈ head.

4 I cry to the Lord with a ˈ loud ˈ voice:
  and he answers me ˈ from his ˈ holy ˈ hill.

5 I lay myself ˈ down and ˈ sleep:
  I wake again beˈcause the ˈ Lord susˈtains me.

6 Therefore I will not be afraid of the multitudes ˈ of the ˈ nations:
  who have set themselves aˈgainst me · on ˈ every ˈ side.

7 Arise Lord   and deliver me ˈ O my ˈ God:
  for you will strike all my enemies upon the cheek *
    you will ˈ break the ˈ teeth of · the unˈgodly.

8 Deliverance beˈlongs · to the ˈ Lord:
  O let your ˈ blessing · be upˈon your ˈ people.

4

GEORGE J. ELVEY

1 Answer me when I call O | God of · my | righteousness:
 when I was hard-pressed you set me free *
 be gracious to me | now and | hear my | prayer.

2 Sons of men   how long will you turn my | glory · to my | shame:
 how long will you love what is worthless * and | seek | after | lies?

3 Know that the Lord has shown me his | wonder·ful | kindness:
 when I call to the | Lord | he will | hear me.

4 Tremble and | do no | sin:
 commune with your own heart up|on your | bed · and be | still.

5 Offer the sacrifices | that are | right:
 and | put your | trust · in the | Lord.

6 There are many who say   'Who will | show us · any | good?:
 the light of your countenance O | Lord has | gone | from us.'

7 Yet you have given my | heart more | gladness:
 than they have when their corn | wine and | oil in|crease.

8 In peace I will lie | down and | sleep:
 for you alone Lord | make me | dwell in | safety.

6

70

E. RIMBAULT

1 O Lord rebuke me not in your | indig|nation:
  nor chasten me | in your | fierce dis|pleasure.

2 Have mercy upon me O Lord for | I am | weak:
  O Lord heal me for my | very | bones · are a|fraid.

3 My soul also is | greatly | troubled:
  and you Lord how | long will | you de|lay?

4 Turn again O Lord and de|liver · my | soul:
  O save me | for your | mercy's | sake.

5 For in death | no man · re|members you:
  and who can | give you | thanks · from the | grave?

6 I am wearied | with my | groaning:
  every night I drown my bed with weeping * and | water · my | couch · with my | tears.

7 My eyes waste a|way for | sorrow:
  they grow dim be|cause of | all my | enemies.

71

GEORGE A. MACFARREN

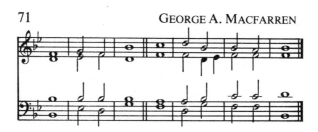

8 Away from me all | you that · do | evil:
  for the Lord has | heard the | voice · of my | weeping.

9 The Lord has heard my | suppli|cation:
  the | Lord · will re|ceive my | prayer.

10 All my enemies shall be put to shame and | greatly · dis|mayed:
  they shall turn back and be con|founded | in a | moment.

8

72

FREDERICK A. G. OUSELEY

UNISON

1 O ' Lord our ' Governor:
how glorious is your ' name in ' all the ' earth!

2 Your majesty above the heavens is ' yet re'counted:
by the ' mouths of ' babes and ' sucklings.

3 You have founded a strong defence a'gainst your ' adversaries:
to quell the ' ene·my ' and · the a'venger.

4 When I consider your heavens the ' work of · your ' fingers:
the moon and the stars which ' you have ' set in ' order,

5 What is man   that you should be ' mindful ' of him:
or the son of ' man that ' you should ' care for him?

6 Yet you have made him little ' less · than a ' god:
and have ' crowned him · with ' glory · and ' honour.

7 You have made him the ' master · of your ' handiwork:
and have put all things in sub'jection · be'neath his ' feet.

8 All ' sheep and ' oxen:
and all the ' creatures ' of the ' field,

9 The birds of the air and the ' fish · of the ' sea:
and everything that moves in the pathways ' of the ' great ' waters.

UNISON
with
Descant

10 O ' Lord our ' Governor:
how glorious is your ' name in ' all the ' earth!

10

JOSEPH BARNBY

1 Why do you stand far ˈ off O ˈ Lord:
  why do you hide your ˈ face in ˈ time of ˈ need?

2 The ungodly in their pride ˈ persecute · the ˈ poor:
  let them be caught in the ˈ schemes they ˈ have deˈvised.

3 For the ungodly man boasts of his ˈ heart's deˈsire:
  he grasps at profit   he ˈ spurns · and blasˈphemes the ˈ Lord.

4 He says in his arrogance ˈ 'God will · not aˈvenge':
  'There is no ˈ God' is ˈ all his ˈ thought.

5 He is settled in ˈ all his ˈ ways:
  your statutes O Lord are far above him ˈ and he ˈ does not ˈ see.

6 He snorts defiance at his enemies * he says in his heart 'I shall ˈ never · be ˈ shaken:
  I shall walk seˈcure from ˈ any · man's ˈ curse.'

7 His mouth is full of opˈpression · and deˈceit:
  mischief and ˈ wickedness · lie ˈ under · his ˈ tongue.

8 He skulks aˈbout · in the ˈ villages:
  and ˈ secret·ly ˈ murders · the ˈ innocent.

9 His eyes watch ˈ out · for the ˈ helpless:
  he lurks conˈcealed · like a ˈ lion · in a ˈ thicket.

10 He lies in wait to ˈ seize up·on the ˈ poor:
   he lays hold on the poor man and ˈ drags him ˈ off · in his ˈ net.

11 The upright are crushed and ˈ humbled · beˈfore him:
   and the helpless ˈ fall inˈto his ˈ power.

12 He says in his heart ˈ 'God · has forˈgotten:
   he has covered his ˈ face and ˈ sees ˈ nothing.'

EDWARD J. HOPKINS

13 Arise O Lord God   lift ˈ up your ˈ hand:
      forˈget · not the ˈ poor for ˈ ever.

14 Why should the wicked man ˈ spurn ˈ God:
      why should he say in his heart ˈ 'He will ˈ not aˈvenge'?

15 Surely you see the ˈ trouble · and the ˈ sorrow:
      you look on   and will take it ˈ into · your ˈ own ˈ hands.

16 The helpless commits himˈself to ˈ you:
      for you are the ˈ helper ˈ of the ˈ fatherless.

† 17 Break the ˈ power of · the unˈgodly:
      search out his wickedness ˈ till · it is ˈ found no ˈ more.

18 The Lord is king for ˈ ever · and ˈ ever:
      the heathen have ˈ perished ˈ from his ˈ land.

19 You have heard the longing of the ˈ meek O ˈ Lord:
      you turned your ˈ ear · to their ˈ hearts' deˈsire,

† 20 To help the poor and fatherless ˈ to their ˈ right:
      that men may no more be ˈ terri·fied ˈ from their ˈ land.

11

WILLIAM H. HARRIS

1   In the Lord I have | found my | refuge:
    how then can you say to me * | 'Flee · like a | bird · to the | mountains;

2   'Look how the wicked bend their bows * and notch the arrow up|on the | string:
    to shoot from the | darkness · at the | true of | heart;

3   'If the foundations | are des|troyed:
    what | can the | just man | do?'

4   The Lord is in his holy place * the Lord is en|throned in | heaven:
    his eyes search out * his glance | tries the | children · of | men.

5   He tries the | righteous · and the | wicked:
    and him that delights in | violence · his | soul ab|hors.

6   He will rain down coals of fire and brimstone up|on the | wicked:
    a scorching wind shall | be their | cup to | drink.

† 7   For the Lord is righteous and loves | righteous | acts:
    the | upright · shall | see his | face.

13

76   WILLIAM CROTCH

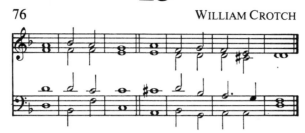

1   How long O Lord will you so | utterly · for|get me:
      how long will you | hide your | face | from me?

2   How long must I suffer anguish in my soul *
      and be so grieved in my heart | day and | night:
      how long shall my | ene·my | triumph | over me?

3   Look upon me O Lord my | God and | answer me:
      lighten my | eyes · lest I | sleep in | death;

4   Lest my enemy say   'I have pre|vailed a|gainst him':
      lest my foes ex|ult | at my | overthrow.

77   JONATHAN BATTISHILL

5   Yet I put my trust in your un|failing | love:
      O let my heart re|joice in | your sal|vation.

6   And I will make my | song · to the | Lord:
      because he | deals so | bounti·fully | with me.

14

JAMES TURLE

1 The fool has said in his heart 'There ˡ is no ˡ God':
    they have all become vile and abominable in their doings *
        there ˡ is not ˡ one that · does ˡ good.

2 The Lord looked down from heaven upon the ˡ children · of ˡ men:
    to see if there were any who would act ˡ wisely · and ˡ seek · after ˡ God.

† 3 But they have all turned out of the way * they have all alike beˡcome corˡrupt:
    there is none that does ˡ good ˡ no not ˡ one.

4 Are all the evildoers devoid of ˡ underˡstanding:
    who eat up my people as men eat bread and ˡ do not ˡ pray · to the ˡ Lord?

5 They shall be ˡ struck with ˡ terror:
    for God is with the ˡ compa·ny ˡ of the ˡ righteous.

6 Though they frustrate the poor man ˡ in his ˡ hopes:
    surely the ˡ Lord ˡ is his ˡ refuge.

7 O that deliverance for Israel might come ˡ forth from ˡ Zion:
    when the Lord turns again the fortunes of his people *
        then shall Jacob reˡjoice and ˡ Israel · be ˡ glad.

15

SAMUEL ARNOLD

1 Lord who may a⎮bide in · your ⎮ tabernacle:
   or who may dwell up⎮on your ⎮ holy ⎮ hill?

2 He that leads an uncorrupt life * and does the ⎮ thing · which is ⎮ right:
   who speaks the truth from his heart * and has not ⎮ slandered ⎮ with his ⎮ tongue;

3 He that has done no evil ⎮ to his ⎮ fellow:
   nor vented a⎮buse a⎮gainst his ⎮ neighbour;

4 In whose eyes the worthless ⎮ have no ⎮ honour:
   but he makes much of ⎮ those that ⎮ fear the ⎮ Lord;

5 He that has ⎮ sworn · to his ⎮ neighbour:
   and will ⎮ not go ⎮ back · on his ⎮ oath;

6 He that has not put his ⎮ money · to ⎮ usury:
   nor taken a ⎮ bribe a⎮gainst the ⎮ innocent.

7 He that ⎮ does these ⎮ things:
   shall ⎮ never · be ⎮ over⎮thrown.

16

JAMES TURLE

1 Preserve | me O | God:
    for in | you · have I | taken | refuge.

2 I have said to the Lord | You are | my lord:
    and all my | good de|pends on | you.

3 As for those who are held | holy · on the | earth:
    the other | gods · in whom | men de|light,

4 Though the idols are many that | men run | after:
    their offerings of blood I will not offer * nor take their | name up|on my | lips.

5 The Lord is my appointed portion | and my | cup:
    you | hold my | lot · in your | hands.

6 The share that has fallen to me is in | pleasant | places:
    and a fair | land is | my pos|session.

7 I will bless the Lord who has | given · me | counsel:
    at night also | he · has in|structed · my | heart.

8 I have set the Lord | always · be|fore me:
    he is at my right | hand · and I | shall not | fall.

† 9 Therefore my heart is glad and my | spirit · re|joices:
    my flesh | also · shall | rest se|cure.

10 For you will not give me over to the | power of | death:
    nor suffer your | faithful one · to | see the | Pit.

11 You will show me the | path of | life:
    in your presence is the fulness of joy *
        and from your right hand flow de|lights for | ever|more.

18

JOHN GOSS

1 I love you O | Lord my | strength:
  O Lord my crag my | fortress · and | my de|liverer,

2 My God   the rock to which I | come for | refuge:
  my shield my mighty saviour | and my | high de|fence.

† 3 I called to the Lord with | loud · lamen|tation:
  and I was | rescued | from my | enemies.

4 The waves of | death en|compassed me:
  and the floods of | chaos | over|whelmed me;

5 The cords of the grave | tightened · a|bout me:
  and the snares of | death lay | in my | path.

6 In my anguish I | called · to the | Lord:
  I cried for | help | to my | God.

7 From his temple he | heard my | voice:
  and my cry came | even | to his | ears.

8 The earth heaved and quaked * the foundations of the | hills were | shaken:
  they | trembled · be|cause · he was | angry.

9 Smoke went | out · from his | nostrils:
  and a consuming | fire | from his | mouth.

10 He parted the heavens and | came | down:
  and there was | darkness | under · his | feet.

11 He rode upon the | cherubim · and | flew:
  he came swooping up|on the | wings · of the | wind.

12 He made the | darkness · his | covering:
  and his canopy was thick | cloud and | water·y | darkness.

13 Out of his clouds   from the | brightness · be|fore him:
  broke | hailstones · and | coals of | fire.

14 The Lord | thundered · in the | heavens:
  the Most | High | uttered · his | voice.

continued

81

John Goss

15 He let loose his arrows   he scattered them on ⁺ every ⁺ side:
    he hurled down ⁺ lightnings · with the ⁺ roar · of the ⁺ thunderbolt.

16 The springs of the ⁺ sea · were un⁺covered:
    and the found⁺ations · of the ⁺ world laid ⁺ bare,

17 At your re⁺buke O ⁺ Lord:
    at the blast of the ⁺ breath of ⁺ your dis⁺pleasure.

82

Thomas A. Walmisley

18 He reached down from on ⁺ high and ⁺ took me:
    he drew me ⁺ out of · the ⁺ great ⁺ waters.

19 He delivered me from my ⁺ strongest ⁺ enemy:
    from my ⁺ foes · that were ⁺ mightier · than ⁺ I.

20 They confronted me in the ⁺ day of · my cal⁺amity:
    but the ⁺ Lord was ⁺ my up⁺holder.

21 He brought me out into a ⁺ place of ⁺ liberty:
    and rescued me be⁺cause · I de⁺lighted · his ⁺ heart.

22 The Lord rewarded me for my ⁺ righteous ⁺ dealing:
    he recompensed me according to the ⁺ cleanness ⁺ of my ⁺ hands,

23 Because I had kept to the ⁺ ways · of the ⁺ Lord:
    and had not turned from my ⁺ God to ⁺ do ⁺ evil.

24 For I had an eye to ⁺ all his ⁺ laws:
    and did not ⁺ put · his com⁺mandments ⁺ from me.

25 I was also ⁺ blameless · be⁺fore him:
    and I kept my⁺self from ⁺ wrong⁺doing.

† 26 Therefore the Lord re⁺warded · my ⁺ innocence:
    because my hands were ⁺ unde⁺filed · in his ⁺ sight.

27 With the faithful you | show your·self | faithful:
   with the | blameless · you | show your·self | blameless;

28 With the | pure · you are | pure:
   but with the | crookèd · you | show yourself · per|verse.

29 For you will save a | humble | people:
   but you bring down the | high looks | of the | proud.

30 You light my lamp O | Lord my | God:
   you make my | darkness | to be | bright.

† 31 For with your help I can charge a | troop of | men:
   with the help of my God I can | leap a | city | wall.

81

JOHN GOSS

32 The way of our God is perfect * the word of the Lord has been | tried · in the | fire:
   he is a shield to | all that | trust in | him.

33 For who is | God · but the | Lord:
   or who is our | rock | but our | God?

34 It is God that | girded me · with | strength:
   that | made my | way | perfect.

35 He made my feet like the | feet · of a | hind:
   and set me sure|footed · up|on the | mountains.

36 He taught my | hands to | fight:
   and my arms to | aim an | arrow · of | bronze.

37 You gave me the shield of | your sal|vation:
   your right hand upheld me * and your swift res|ponse has | made me | great.

38 You lengthened my | stride be|neath me:
   and my | ankles | did not | slip.

39 I pursued my enemies and | over|took them:
   nor did I turn again | till · I had | made an | end of them.

19

RICHARD WOODWARD

1 The heavens declare the | glory · of | God:
    and the | firmament · pro|claims his | handiwork;

2 One day | tells it · to an|other:
    and night to | night com|muni·cates | knowledge.

3 There is no | speech or | language:
    nor | are their | voices | heard;

4 Yet their sound has gone out through | all the | world:
    and their | words · to the | ends · of the | earth.

5 There he has pitched a | tent · for the | sun:
    which comes out as a bridegroom from his chamber *
        and rejoices like a | strong · man to | run his | course.

6 Its rising is at one end of the heavens * and its circuit to their | farthest | bound:
    and nothing is | hidden | from its | heat.

84

W. TURNER

7 The law of the Lord is perfect re|viving · the | soul:
    the command of the Lord is true | and makes | wise the | simple.

8 The precepts of the Lord are right and re|joice the | heart:
    the commandment of the Lord is pure | and gives | light · to the | eyes.

9 The fear of the Lord is clean and en|dures for | ever:
    the judgements of the Lord are unchanging and | righteous | every | one.

10 More to be desired are they than gold * even | much fine | gold:
    sweeter also than honey * than the | honey · that | drips · from the | comb.

11 Moreover by them is your | servant | taught:
    and in keeping them | there is | great re|ward.

12 Who can know his own un|witting | sins?:
    O cleanse me | from my | secret | faults.

13 Keep your servant also from presumptuous sins * lest they get the | master·y | over me:
    so I shall be clean and | innocent · of | great of|fence.

14 May the words of my mouth and the meditation of my heart *
        be acceptable | in your | sight:
    O Lord my | strength and | my re|deemer.

20

85   GERALD H. KNIGHT

1 May the Lord hear you in the | day of | trouble:
   the God of Jacob | lift you | up to | safety.

2 May he send you his | help · from the | sanctuary:
   and be your | strong sup|port from | Zion.

3 May he remember | all your | offerings:
   and accept with | favour · your | burnt | sacrifices,

4 Grant you your | heart's de|sire:
   and ful|fil | all your | purposes.

† 5 May we also rejoice in your victory * and triumph in the | name of · our | God:
     the Lord per|form all | your pe|titions.

6 Now I know that the Lord will | save · his a|nointed:
   that he will answer him from his holy heaven *
       with the victorious | strength · of his | right | hand.

7 Some put their trust in chariots and | some in | horses:
   but we will trust in the | name · of the | Lord our | God.

8 They are brought | down and | fallen:
   but we are made | strong and | stand | upright.

9 O Lord | save the | king:
   and hear us | when we | call up|on you.

JOHN GOSS

1   The king shall rejoice in your ' strength O ' Lord:
      he shall ex'ult in ' your sal'vation.

2   You have given him his ' heart's de'sire:
      you have not de'nied him · the re'quest · of his ' lips.

3   For you came to meet him with the ' blessings · of suc'cess:
      and placed a crown of ' gold up'on his ' head.

4   He asked you for ' life · and you ' gave it him:
      length of ' days for ' ever · and ' ever.

5   Great is his glory because of ' your sal'vation:
      you have ' clothed him · with ' honour · and ' majesty.

6   You have given him ever'lasting · fe'licity:
      and made him ' glad · with the ' joy of · your ' presence.

† 7   For the king puts his ' trust · in the ' Lord:
      and through the tender mercy of the Most High ' he shall ' never · be ' moved.

8   Your hand shall light up'on your ' enemies:
      and your right hand shall ' find out ' all who ' hate you.

9   You will make them like a blazing furnace in the ' day of · your ' coming:
      the Lord will overwhelm them in his wrath and ' fire ' shall con'sume them.

10   You will root out their offspring ' from the ' earth:
      and their seed from a'mong the ' children · of ' men;

11   Because they have stirred up ' evil · a'gainst you:
      and plotted mischief ' which they ' cannot · per'form.

12   Therefore will you set your ' shoulder · to'ward them:
      and draw the string of the ' bow to ' strike at · their ' faces.

13   Arise O Lord in your ' great ' strength:
      and we will ' sing and ' praise your ' power.

22

MATTHEW CAMIDGE

1 My God my God   why have ˈ you forˈsaken me:
  why are you so far from helping me * and from the ˈ words ˈ of my ˈ groaning?

2 My God I cry to you by day   but you ˈ do not ˈ answer:
  and by night ˈ also · I ˈ take no ˈ rest.

3 But you conˈtinue ˈ holy:
  you that ˈ are the ˈ praise of ˈ Israel.

4 In you our ˈ fathers ˈ trusted:
  they ˈ trusted · and ˈ you deˈlivered them;

5 To you they cried and ˈ they were ˈ saved:
  they put their trust in you ˈ and were ˈ not conˈfounded.

6 But as for me   I am a worm and ˈ no ˈ man:
  the scorn of ˈ men · and deˈspised · by the ˈ people.

7 All those that see me ˈ laugh me · to ˈ scorn:
  they shoot out their lips at me and ˈ wag their ˈ heads ˈ saying,

8 'He trusted in the Lord   ˈ let him · deˈliver him:
  let him deˈliver him · if ˈ he deˈlights in him.'

9 But you are he that took me ˈ out of · the ˈ womb:
  that brought me to lie at ˈ peace · on my ˈ mother's ˈ breast.

10 On you have I been cast ˈ since my ˈ birth:
   you are my God ˈ even · from my ˈ mother's ˈ womb.

11 O go not from me   for trouble is ˈ hard at ˈ hand:
   and ˈ there is ˈ none to ˈ help.

12 Many ˈ oxen · surˈround me:
   fat bulls of Bashan close me ˈ in on ˈ every ˈ side.

13 They gape ˈ wide their ˈ mouths at me:
   like ˈ lions · that ˈ roar and ˈ rend.

14 I am poured out like water * and all my bones are ˈ out of ˈ joint:
   my heart within my ˈ breast · is like ˈ melting ˈ wax.

15 My mouth is dried ˈ up · like a ˈ potsherd:
   and my ˈ tongue ˈ clings · to my ˈ gums.

continued

MATTHEW CAMIDGE

16 My hands and my ˈ feet are ˈ withered:
  and you ˈ lay me · in the ˈ dust of ˈ death.

17 For many dogs are ˈ come aˈbout me:
  and a band of evilˈdoers ˈ hem me ˈ in.

18 I can count ˈ all my ˈ bones:
  they stand ˈ staring · and ˈ gazing · upˈon me.

19 They part my ˈ garments · aˈmong them:
  and cast ˈ lots ˈ for my ˈ clothing.

20 O Lord do not ˈ stand far ˈ off:
  you are my helper　ˈ hasten ˈ to my ˈ aid.

21 Deliver my ˈ body · from the ˈ sword:
  my ˈ life · from the ˈ power · of the ˈ dogs;

22 O save me from the ˈ lion's ˈ mouth:
  and my afflicted soul from the ˈ horns · of the ˈ wild ˈ oxen.

MATTHEW CAMIDGE

23 I will tell of your ˈ name · to my ˈ brethren:
  in the midst of the congreˈgation ˈ will I ˈ praise you.

24 O praise the Lord all ˈ you that ˈ fear him:
  hold him in honour O seed of Jacob *
  and let the seed of ˈ Israel ˈ stand in ˈ awe of him.

† 25 For he has not despised nor abhorred the poor man ˈ in his ˈ misery:
  nor did he hide his face from him * but ˈ heard him ˈ when he ˈ cried.

26 From you springs my praise in the ˈ great · congreˈgation:
  I will pay my vows in the ˈ sight of ˈ all that ˈ fear you;

27 The meek shall eat of the sacrifice ˈ and be ˈ satisfied:
  and those who seek the Lord shall praise him * may their ˈ hearts reˈjoice for ˈ ever!

28 Let all the ends of the earth remember and | turn · to the | Lord:
and let all the families of the | nations | worship · be|fore him.

29 For the kingdom | is the | Lord's:
and he shall be | ruler | over · the | nations.

23

89

THOMAS A. WALMISLEY

90   JAMES TURLE

1 The Lord | is my | shepherd:
therefore | can I | lack | nothing.

2 He will make me lie down in | green | pastures:
and | lead me · be|side still | waters.

3 He will re|fresh my | soul:
and guide me in right pathways | for his | name's | sake.

4 Though I walk through the valley of the shadow of death   I will | fear no | evil:
for you are with me * your | rod · and your | staff | comfort me.

5 You spread a table before me * in the face of | those who | trouble me:
you have anointed my head with oil | and my | cup · will be | full.

6 Surely your goodness and loving-kindness will follow me * all the | days · of my | life:
and I shall dwell in the | house · of the | Lord for | ever.

24

JOSEPH BARNBY

92

GEORGE THALBEN-BALL

Unison or Harmony

for verses
7 and 9

1 The earth is the Lord's and | all · that is | in it:
   the compass of the | world and | those who | dwell therein.

2 For he has founded it up|on the | seas:
   and es|tablished it · up|on the | waters.

3 Who shall ascend the | hill · of the | Lord:
   or who shall | stand · in his | holy | place?

4 He that has clean hands and a | pure | heart:
   who has not set his soul upon idols * nor | sworn his | oath · to a | lie.

5 He shall receive | blessing · from the | Lord:
   and recompense from the | God of | his sal|vation.

6 Of such a kind as this are | those who | seek him:
   those who seek your | face O | God of | Jacob.

Men only   7 Lift up your heads O you gates * and be lifted up you ever|lasting | doors:
   and the King of | glory | shall come | in.

Trebles only   8 Who is the | King of | glory?:

Full Harmony   the Lord strong and mighty * the | Lord | mighty · in | battle.

Men only   9 Lift up your heads O you gates * and be lifted up you ever|lasting | doors:
   and the King of | glory | shall come | in.

Trebles only   10 Who is the | King of | glory?:

Full Harmony   the Lord of hosts | he · is the | King of | glory.

25

E. EDWARDS

1 In you O Lord my God have I ∣ put my ∣ hope:
    in you have I trusted   let me not be ashamed *
    nor let my ∣ ene·mies ∣ triumph ∣ over me.

2 Let none who wait for you be ∣ put to ∣ shame:
    but let those that break faith be con∣founded · and ∣ gain ∣ nothing.

3 Show me your ∣ ways O ∣ Lord:
    and ∣ teach me ∣ your ∣ paths.

4 Lead me in the ways of your ∣ truth and ∣ teach me:
    for you are the ∣ God of ∣ my sal∣vation.

5 In you have I hoped ∣ all the · day ∣ long:
    be∣cause of · your ∣ goodness · O ∣ Lord.

6 Call to mind your compassion and your ∣ loving-∣kindness:
    for ∣ they are ∣ from of ∣ old.

7 Remember not the sins of my youth nor ∣ my trans∣gressions:
    but according ∣ to your ∣ mercy ∣ think on me.

8 Good and upright ∣ is the ∣ Lord:
    therefore will he direct ∣ sinners ∣ in the ∣ way.

† 9 The meek he will guide in the ∣ path of ∣ justice:
    and ∣ teach the ∣ humble · his ∣ ways.

10 All the paths of the Lord are ∣ faithful · and ∣true:
    for those who keep his ∣ covenant · and ∣ his com∣mandments.

11 For your name's ∣ sake O ∣ Lord:
    be merciful to my ∣ sin though ∣ it is ∣ great.

12 Who is he that ∣ fears the ∣ Lord?:
    him will the Lord direct in the ∣ way that ∣ he should ∣ choose.

13 His soul shall ∣ dwell at ∣ ease:
    and his ∣ children · shall in∣herit · the ∣ land.

14 The confidences of God belong to ∣ those that ∣ fear him:
    and his covenant shall ∣ give them ∣ under∣standing.

15 My eyes are ever ∣ looking · to the ∣ Lord:
    for he will bring my ∣ feet ∣ out of · the ∣ net.

continued

E. Edwards

16 Turn your face toward me | and be | gracious:
   for | I am · a|lone · and in | misery.

17 O free my | heart from | pain:
   and bring me | out of | my dis|tress.

18 Give heed to my af|fliction · and ad|versity:
   and for|give me | all my | sins.

19 Consider my enemies how | many · they | are:
   and they bear a | vio·lent | hate a|gainst me.

20 O keep my | life · and de|liver me:
   put me not to shame   for I | come to | you for | refuge.

21 Let innocence and integrity | be my | guard:
   for in | you | have I | hoped.

† 22 O God de|liver | Israel:
   out of | all his | tribu|lation.

26

EDMUND CHIPP

1 Give judgement for me O Lord * for I have walked in ǀ my inǀtegrity:
   I have trusted in the ǀ Lord and ǀ not ǀ wavered.

2 Put me to the test O ǀ Lord and ǀ prove me:
   try my ǀ mind ǀ and my ǀ heart.

3 For your steadfast love has been ever beǀfore my ǀ eyes:
   and ǀ I have ǀ walked in · your ǀ truth.

4 I have not ǀ sat · with deǀceivers:
   nor conǀsorted ǀ with the ǀ hypocrites;

5 I hate the asǀsembly · of the ǀ wicked:
   I will not ǀ sit ǀ with the · unǀgodly.

6 I wash my hands in ǀ innocence · O ǀ Lord:
   that I may ǀ go aǀbout your ǀ altar,

† 7 And lift up the ǀ voice of ǀ thanksgiving:
   to tell of ǀ all your ǀ marvel·lous ǀ works.

8 Lord I love the house of your ǀ habitǀation:
   and the ǀ place · where your ǀ glory ǀ dwells.

9 Do not sweep me aǀway with ǀ sinners:
   nor my ǀ life with ǀ men of ǀ blood,

10 In whose hand is aǀbominǀation:
   and their right ǀ hand is ǀ full of ǀ bribes.

11 As for me   I walk in ǀ my inǀtegrity:
   O ransom me ǀ and be ǀ favourable · toǀward me.

† 12 My foot stands on an ǀ even ǀ path:
   I will bless the ǀ Lord · in the ǀ great · congreǀgation.

27

JOHN LEMON

1 The Lord is my light and my salvation * whom then | shall I | fear?:
   the Lord is the stronghold of my life * of whom | shall I | be a|fraid?

2 When the wicked   even my enemies and my foes * come upon me | to de|vour me:
   they shall | stumble | and | fall.

3 If an army encamp against me * my heart shall | not · be a|fraid:
   and if war should rise a|gainst me | yet · will I | trust.

4 One thing I have asked from the Lord which I | will re|quire:
   that I may dwell in the house of the Lord | all the | days · of my | life,

† 5 To see the fair | beauty · of the | Lord:
   and to | seek his | will · in his | temple.

6 For he will hide me under his shelter in the | day of | trouble:
   and conceal me in the shadow of his tent * and set me | high up|on a | rock.

7 And now he will lift | up my | head:
   above my | ene·mies | round a|bout me.

† 8 And I will offer sacrifices in his sanctuary with | exul|tation:
   I will sing   I will sing | praises | to the | Lord.

STEPHEN ELVEY

9 O Lord hear my | voice · when I | cry:
   have | mercy · up|on me · and | answer me.

10 My heart has said of you | 'Seek his | face':
   your | face Lord | I will | seek.

11 Do not | hide your | face from me:
   or thrust your | servant · a|side · in dis|pleasure;

12 For you have ᐧ been my ᐧ helper:
    do not cast me away or forsake me O ᐧ God of ᐧ my salᐧvation.

† 13 Though my father and my ᐧ mother · forᐧsake me:
    the ᐧ Lord will ᐧ take me ᐧ up.

14 Teach me your ᐧ way O ᐧ Lord:
    and lead me in an even path ᐧ for they ᐧ lie in ᐧ wait for me.

15 Do not give me over to the ᐧ will of · my ᐧ enemies:
    for false witnesses have risen against me * and ᐧ those who ᐧ breathe out ᐧ violence.

16 But I believe that I shall surely see the ᐧ goodness · of the ᐧ Lord:
    in the ᐧ land ᐧ of the ᐧ living.

17 O wait for the Lord * stand firm and he will ᐧ strengthen · your ᐧ heart:
    and ᐧ wait I ᐧ say · for the ᐧ Lord.

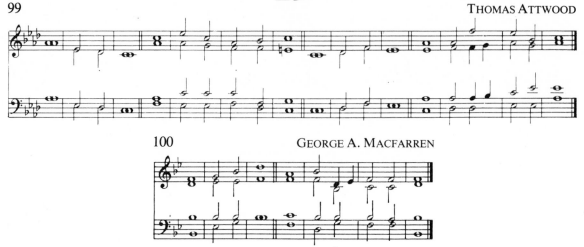

99 THOMAS ATTWOOD

100 GEORGE A. MACFARREN

1 Ascribe to the Lord you ǀ sons of ǀ heaven:
  ascribe to the ǀ Lord ǀ glory · and ǀ might.

2 Ascribe to the Lord the honour ǀ due · to his ǀ name:
  O worship the Lord in the ǀ beauty ǀ of his ǀ holiness.

3 The voice of the Lord is upǀon the ǀ waters:
  the God of glory thunders the Lord upǀon the ǀ great ǀ waters.

4 The voice of the Lord is mighty in ǀ operǀation:
  the voice of the ǀ Lord · is a ǀ glori·ous ǀ voice.

5 The voice of the Lord ǀ breaks the ǀ cedar-trees:
  the Lord breaks in ǀ pieces · the ǀ cedars · of ǀ Lebanon.

6 He makes them ǀ skip · like a ǀ calf:
  Lebanon and Sirion ǀ like a ǀ young wild ǀ ox.

7 The voice of the Lord diǀvides the ǀ lightning-flash:
  the voice of the Lord whirls the sands of the desert *
   the Lord ǀ whirls the ǀ desert · of ǀ Kadesh.

8 The voice of the Lord rends the terebinth trees * and strips ǀ bare the ǀ forests:
  in his ǀ temple ǀ all cry ǀ 'Glory'.

9 The Lord sits enthroned aǀbove the ǀ water-flood:
  the Lord sits enǀthroned · as a ǀ king for ǀ ever.

10 The Lord will give ǀ strength · to his ǀ people:
  the Lord will give to his ǀ people · the ǀ blessing · of ǀ peace.

30

JAMES TURLE

1   I will exalt you O Lord * for you have drawn me | up · from the | depths:
     and have not suffered my | foes to | triumph | over me.

2   O Lord my | God I | cried to you:
     and | you have | made me | whole.

† 3   You brought me back O Lord from the | land of | silence:
     you saved my life from among | those that · go | down · to the | Pit.

4   Sing praises to the Lord all | you his | faithful ones:
     and give | thanks · to his | holy | name.

5   For if in his anger is havoc * in his good | favour · is | life:
     heaviness may endure for a night * but | joy comes | in the | morning.

6   In my prosperity I said   'I shall | never · be | moved:
     your goodness O Lord has | set me · on so | firm a | hill.'

7   Then you | hid your | face from me:
     and | I was | greatly · dis|mayed.

8   I cried to | you O | God:
     and made my petition | humbly | to my | Lord.

9   'What profit is there in my blood * if I go | down · to the | Pit:
     can the dust give you thanks | or de|clare your | faithfulness?

† 10   'Hear O | Lord · and be | merciful:
     O | Lord | be my | helper.'

11   You have turned my lamentation | into | dancing:
     you have put off my sackcloth and | girded | me with | joy,

12   That my heart may sing your praise and | never · be | silent:
     O Lord my God   I will | give you | thanks for | ever.

31

WILLIAM CROTCH

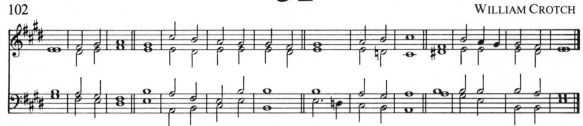

1 To you Lord have I ˈ come for ˈ shelter:
   let me ˈ never · be ˈ put to ˈ shame.

2 O deliver me ˈ in your ˈ righteousness:
   incline your ear to me ˈ and be ˈ swift to ˈ save me.

3 Be for me a rock of refuge   a fortress ˈ to deˈfend me:
   for you are my ˈ high rock ˈ and my ˈ stronghold.

4 Lead me and guide me for your ˈ name's ˈ sake:
   bring me out of the net that they have secretly laid for me *
   for ˈ you ˈ are my ˈ strength.

5 Into your hands I comˈmit my ˈ spirit:
   you will redeem me ˈ O Lord ˈ God of ˈ truth.

6 I hate those that ˈ clutch vain ˈ idols:
   but my ˈ trust is ˈ in the ˈ Lord.

7 I will rejoice and be glad in your ˈ loving-ˈkindness:
   for you have looked on my distress * and ˈ known me ˈ in adˈversity.

8 You have not given me over to the ˈ power · of the ˈ enemy:
   you have set my feet where ˈ I may ˈ walk at ˈ liberty.

WILLIAM CROTCH

9 Have mercy upon me O Lord   for ˈ I am · in ˈ trouble:
   my eye wastes away for grief * my throat also ˈ and my ˈ inward ˈ parts.

10 For my life wears out in sorrow and my ˈ years with ˈ sighing:
   my strength fails me in my affliction * and my ˈ bones ˈ are conˈsumed.

11 I am become the scorn of ˈ all my ˈ enemies:
   and my neighbours ˈ wag their ˈ heads · in deˈrision.

12 I am a thing of | horror · to my | friends:
and those that see me in the | street | shrink | from me.

13 I am forgotten like a dead man | out of | mind:
I have be|come · like a | broken | vessel.

14 For I hear the | whispering · of | many:
and | fear · is on | every | side;

15 While they plot to|gether · a|gainst me:
and scheme to | take a|way my | life.

16 But in you Lord have I | put my | trust:
I have said | 'You | are my | God.'

17 All my days are | in your | hand:
O deliver me from the power of my | enemies · and | from my | persecutors.

18 Make your face to shine up|on your | servant:
and save me | for your | mercy's | sake.

19 O Lord let me not be confounded * for I have | called up|on you:
but let the wicked be put to shame * and brought to | silence | in the | grave.

20 Let the lying | lips be | dumb:
that in pride and contempt speak such | insolence · a|gainst the | just.

102   WILLIAM CROTCH

21 O how plentiful is your goodness * stored up for | those that | fear you:
and prepared in the sight of men * for all who | come to | you for | refuge.

22 You will hide them in the cover of your presence from the | plots of | men:
you will shelter them in your refuge | from the | strife of | tongues.

23 Blessèd be the | Lord our | God:
for he has wonderfully shown me his steadfast love *
when I was | as a | city · be|sieged.

24 When I was afraid I | said in · my | haste:
'I am | cut off | from your | sight.'

25 But you heard the voice of my | suppli|cation:
when I | cried to | you for | help.

26 Love the Lord all | you his | faithful ones:
for the Lord guards the true * but | fully · re|quites the | proud.

† 27 Be strong   and let your | heart take | courage:
all | you that | hope · in the | Lord.

32

JOHN JONES

1 Blessèd is he whose | sin · is for|given:
  whose in|iquity · is | put a|way.

2 Blessèd is the man to whom the Lord im|putes no | blame:
  and in whose | spirit · there | is no | guile.

3 For whilst I | held my | tongue:
  my bones wasted a|way · with my | daily · com|plaining.

4 Your hand was heavy upon me | day and | night:
  and my moisture was dried | up · like a | drought in | summer.

5 Then I ack|nowledged · my | sin to you:
  and my in|iquity · I | did not | hide;

6 I said   'I will confess my trans|gressions · to the | Lord':
  and so you forgave the | wicked·ness | of my | sin.

7 For this cause shall everyone that is faithful make his prayer to you *
      in the | day of | trouble:
  and in the time of the great water-floods | they shall | not come | near him.

8 You are a place to hide me in * you will pre|serve me · from | trouble:
  you will surround me with de|liverance · on | every | side.

9 'I will instruct you * and direct you in the way that | you should | go:
  I will fasten my eye up|on you · and | give you | counsel.

10 'Be not like horse or mule that have no | under|standing:
   whose forward course must be | curbed with | bit and | bridle.'

11 Great tribulations remain | for the · un|godly:
   but whoever puts his trust in the Lord * mercy em|braces him · on | every | side.

12 Rejoice in the Lord you righteous | and be | glad:
   and shout for joy all | you · that are | true of | heart.

33

JAMES TURLE

1　Rejoice in the | Lord you | righteous:
　　for it be|fits the | just to | praise him.

2　Give the Lord thanks up|on the | harp:
　　and sing his praise to the | lute of | ten | strings.

3　O sing him a | new | song:
　　make sweetest | melody · with | shouts of | praise.

4　For the word of the | Lord is | true:
　　and | all his | works are | faithful.

5　He loves | righteousness · and | justice:
　　the earth is filled with the loving-|kindness | of the | Lord.

6　By the word of the Lord were the | heavens | made:
　　and their numberless | stars · by the | breath of · his | mouth.

7　He gathered the waters of the sea as | in a | water-skin:
　　and laid up the | deep | in his | treasuries.

8　Let the whole earth | fear the | Lord:
　　and let all the inhabitants of the | world | stand in | awe of him.

9　For he spoke and | it was | done:
　　he commanded | and it | stood | fast.

10　The Lord frustrates the | counsels · of the | nations:
　　he brings to nothing the de|vices | of the | peoples.

11　But the counsels of the Lord shall en|dure for | ever:
　　the purposes of his heart from gener|ation · to | gener|ation.

12　Blessèd is that nation whose | God · is the | Lord:
　　the people he chose to | be his | own pos|session.

.13　The Lord looks down from heaven * and surveys all the | children · of | men:
　　he considers from his dwelling-place all the in|habit·ants | of the | earth;

14　He who fashioned the | hearts of · them | all:
　　and compre|hends all | that they | do.

15　A king is not saved by a | mighty | army:
　　nor is a warrior de|livered · by | much | strength;

continued

JAMES TURLE

16 A horse is a vain hope to | save a | man:
    nor can he rescue | any · by his | great | power.

17 But the eye of the Lord is on | those that | fear him:
    on those that trust in | his un|failing | love,

18 To de|liver them · from | death:
    and to | feed them · in the | time of | dearth.

19 We have waited eagerly | for the | Lord:
    for | he is · our | help · and our | shield.

20 Surely our hearts shall re|joice in | him:
    for we have | trusted · in his | holy | name.

† 21 Let your merciful kindness be up|on us · O | Lord:
    even as our | hope | is in | you.

34

FREDERICK A. G. OUSELEY

1 I will bless the | Lord con|tinually:
   his praise shall be | always | in my | mouth.

2 Let my soul | boast · of the | Lord:
   the humble shall | hear it | and re|joice.

3 O praise the | Lord with | me:
   let us ex|alt his | name to|gether.

4 For I sought the Lord's | help · and he | answered:
   and he | freed me · from | all my | fears.

5 Look towards him and be | bright with | joy:
   your | faces · shall | not · be a|shamed.

6 Here is a wretch who cried and the | Lord | heard him:
   and | saved him · from | all his | troubles.

FREDERICK A. G. OUSELEY

7　The angel of the Lord encamps round ' those who ' fear him:
　　and de'livers · them ' in their ' need.

8　O taste and see that the ' Lord is ' good:
　　happy the ' man who ' hides in ' him!

9　Fear the Lord all ' you his ' holy ones:
　　for those who ' fear him ' never ' lack.

10　Lions may suffer ' want · and go ' hungry:
　　but those who seek the ' Lord lack ' nothing ' good.

11　Come my children　' listen · to ' me:
　　and I will ' teach you · the ' fear · of the ' Lord.

12　Which of you ' relish·es ' life:
　　wants ' time · to en'joy good ' things?

13　Keep your ' tongue from ' evil:
　　and your ' lips from ' telling ' lies.

14　Turn from evil and ' do ' good:
　　seek ' peace ' and pur'sue it.

15　The eyes of God are ' on the ' righteous:
　　and his ' ears to'wards their ' cry.

16　The Lord sets his face against ' wrong'doers:
　　to root out their ' memo·ry ' from the ' earth.

17　The righteous cry　the ' Lord ' hears it:
　　and ' frees them · from ' all · their af'flictions.

18　The Lord is close to those who are ' broken-'hearted:
　　and the ' crushed in ' spirit · he ' saves.

19　The trials of the ' righteous · are ' many:
　　but our God de'livers · him ' from them ' all.

20　He guards ' all his ' bones:
　　so ' that not ' one is ' broken.

21　Evil will ' slay the ' wicked:
　　and those who hate the ' righteous · will ' be de'stroyed.

22　The Lord ransoms the ' lives · of his ' servants:
　　and none who hide in ' him will ' be de'stroyed.

36

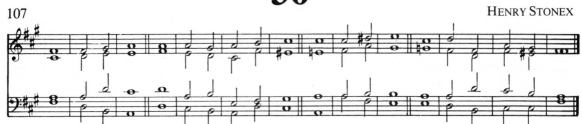

107

HENRY STONEX

1 The transgressor speaks from the wickedness in his ǀ own ǀ heart:
   there is no fear of ǀ God beǀfore his ǀ eyes.

2 For he flatters himself in his ǀ own ǀ sight:
   he hates his inǀiquity · to be ǀ found ǀ out.

3 The words of his mouth are wickedness ǀ and deǀceit:
   he has ceased to act ǀ wisely · and ǀ do ǀ good.

4 He plots mischief as he lies upǀon his ǀ bed:
   he has set himself on a path that is not good * he ǀ does not ǀ spurn ǀ evil.

108

WILLIAM JACKSON

5 Your unfailing kindness O Lord is ǀ in the ǀ heavens:
   and your faithfulness ǀ reaches ǀ to the ǀ clouds.

6 Your righteousness is like the ǀ strong ǀ mountains:
   and your justice as the great deep * you O Lord ǀ save both ǀ man and ǀ beast.

7 How precious O God is your enǀduring ǀ kindness:
   the children of men shall take refuge under the ǀ shadow ǀ of your ǀ wings.

8 They shall be satisfied with the good things ǀ of your ǀ house:
   and you will give them drink from the ǀ river · of ǀ your deǀlights.

9 For with you is the ǀ well of ǀ life:
   and in your ǀ light shall ǀ we see ǀ light.

10 O continue your merciful kindness toward ǀ those who ǀ know you:
   and your righteous dealing to ǀ those · that are ǀ true of ǀ heart.

11 Let not the foot of the ǀ proud · come aǀgainst me:
   nor the hand of the unǀgodly ǀ drive · me aǀway.

12 There are they fallen   ǀ those who · do ǀ evil:
   they are thrust down and ǀ shall not ǀ rise aǀgain.

37

JOHN GOSS

1 Do not | vie · with the | wicked:
   or | envy | those that · do | wrong;

2 For they will soon | wither · like the | grass:
   and fade a|way · like the | green | leaf.

3 Trust in the | Lord and · do | good:
   and you shall dwell in the land and | feed in | safe | pastures.

4 Let the Lord be | your de|light:
   and he will | grant you · your | heart's de|sire.

5 Commit your | way · to the | Lord:
   trust | him and | he will | act.

6 He will make your righteousness shine as | clear · as the | light:
   and your | inno·cence | as the | noonday.

7 Be still before the Lord * and wait | patient·ly | for him:
   do not be vexed when a man prospers * when he puts his | evil | purposes · to | work.

8 Let go of anger and a|bandon | wrath:
   let not envy | move you · to | do | evil.

9 For the wicked shall be | cut | down:
   but those who wait for the | Lord · shall pos|sess the | land.

10 In a little while the ungodly shall | be no | more:
   you will look for him in his place but | he will | not be | found.

† 11 But the meek shall pos|sess the | land:
   and en|joy · the a|bundance · of | peace.

12 The ungodly man plots a|gainst the | righteous:
   and | gnashes · at him | with his | teeth.

13 But the Lord shall | laugh him · to | scorn:
   for he sees that the | day · for his | overthrow · is | near.

14 The ungodly have drawn the sword and | strung the | bow:
   to strike down the poor and needy * to slaughter | those that | walk in | innocence.

15 Their swords shall pierce their | own | hearts:
   and their | bows | shall be | broken.

continued

JOHN GOSS

16 Though the righteous man | has · but a | little:
it is better than the great | wealth of | the un|godly.

17 For the strong arm of the ungodly | shall be | broken:
but the | Lord up|holds the | righteous.

18 The Lord cares for the | lives · of the | innocent:
and their heritage | shall be | theirs for | ever.

19 They shall not be put to shame in the | evil | days:
but in time of famine | they shall | eat their | fill.

† 20 As for the ungodly they shall perish * they are the enemies | of the | Lord:
like fuel in a furnace they shall | vanish · a|way in | smoke.

110

HENRY J. GAUNTLETT

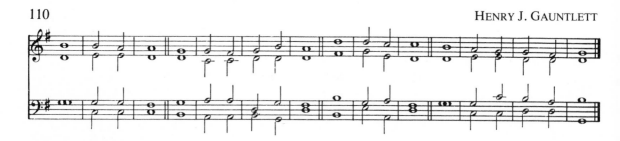

21 The ungodly man borrows but does | not re|pay:
but the | righteous · is | gracious · and | gives.

22 Those who are blessed by God shall pos|sess the | land:
but those whom he has | cursed · shall be | cut | down.

23 If a man's steps are | guided · by the | Lord:
and | he de|lights in · his | way,

24 Though he stumble he shall | not fall | headlong:
for the Lord | holds him | by the | hand.

25 I have been young and | now am | old:
but I never saw the righteous man forsaken * or his | children | begging · their | bread.

26 He is ever | gracious · and | lends:
and his | children | shall be | blessed.

27 Turn from evil and | do | good:
and you shall | dwell · in the | land for | ever.

28 For the ǀ Lord loves ǀ justice:
  he will ǀ not forǀsake his ǀ faithful ones.

29 But the unjust shall be deǀstroyed for ǀ ever:
  and the children of the unǀgodly · shall be ǀ cut ǀ down.

30 The just shall posǀsess the ǀ land:
  and they shall ǀ dwell in ǀ it for ǀ ever.

31 The mouth of the righteous man ǀ utters ǀ wisdom:
  and his ǀ tongue speaks ǀ what is ǀ right.

32 The law of his God is ǀ in his ǀ heart:
  and his ǀ footsteps ǀ will not ǀ slip.

33 The ungodly man watches ǀ out · for the ǀ righteous:
  and ǀ seeks ocǀcasion · to ǀ slay him.

34 But the Lord will not abandon him ǀ to his ǀ power:
  nor let him be conǀdemned when ǀ he is ǀ judged.

† 35 Wait for the Lord and ǀ hold to · his ǀ way:
  and he will raise you up to possess the land *
    to see the unǀgodly · when ǀ they are · deǀstroyed.

36 I have seen the ungodly in ǀ terri·fying ǀ power:
  spreading himself ǀ like a · luxǀuri·ant ǀ tree;

37 I passed by again and ǀ he was ǀ gone:
  I searched for him ǀ but · he could ǀ not be ǀ found.

38 Observe the blameless man and conǀsider · the ǀ upright:
  for the man of ǀ peace shall ǀ have posǀterity.

39 But transgressors shall be deǀstroyed · altoǀgether:
  and the posterity of the ǀ wicked · shall be ǀ cut ǀ down.

40 Deliverance for the righteous shall ǀ come · from the ǀ Lord:
  he is their ǀ strength in ǀ time of ǀ trouble.

41 The Lord will help them ǀ and deǀliver them:
  he will save them from the ungodly and deliver them *
    because they ǀ come to ǀ him for ǀ refuge.

38

CHARLES V. STANFORD

1 O Lord rebuke me not ' in your ' anger:
   nor chasten me ' in your ' fierce dis'pleasure.

2 For your arrows have been ' aimed a'gainst me:
   and your hand has come ' down ' heavy · up'on me.

3 There is no health in my flesh * because of your ' indig'nation:
   nor soundness in my bones by ' reason ' of my ' sin.

4 The tide of my iniquities has gone ' over · my ' head:
   their weight is a burden too ' heavy · for ' me to ' bear.

5 My wounds ' stink and ' fester:
   be'cause ' of my ' foolishness.

6 I am bowed down and ' brought so ' low:
   that I go ' mourning ' all the · day ' long.

7 For my loins are filled with a ' burning ' pain:
   and there is no sound ' part in ' all my ' body.

8 I am numbed and ' stricken · to the ' ground:
   I cry aloud in the ' yearning ' of my ' heart.

9 O Lord   all I long for ' is be'fore you:
   and my deep sighing ' is not ' hidden ' from you.

10 My heart is in tumult   my ' strength ' fails me:
   and even the ' light of · my ' eyes has ' gone from me.

11 My friends and my companions hold aloof from ' my af'fliction:
   and my ' kinsmen ' stand far ' off.

12 Those who seek my ' life ' strike at me:
   and those that desire my hurt spread evil tales * and murmur ' slanders ' all the ' day.

13 But I am like a deaf man and ' hear ' nothing:
   like one that is dumb who ' does not ' open · his ' mouth.

14 So I have become as one who ' cannot ' hear:
   in whose ' mouth · there is ' no re'tort.

15 For in you Lord have I ' put my ' trust:
   and you will ' answer me · O ' Lord my ' God.

111 CHARLES V. STANFORD

16 For I prayed   'Let them never ex|ult | over me:
those who turn arrogant | when my | foot | slips.'

17 Truly I am | ready · to | fall:
and my | pain is | with me · con|tinually.

18 But I ac|knowledge · my | wickedness:
and I am filled with | sorrow | at my | sin.

19 Those that are my enemies without cause are | great in | number:
and those who hate me | wrongful|ly are | many.

20 Those also who repay evil for good | are a|gainst me:
because I | seek | after | good.

† 21 Forsake me not O Lord * go not far | from me · my | God:
hasten to my | help O | Lord · my sal|vation.

39

JOSEPH BARNBY

1 I said 'I will keep watch over my ways * lest I | sin · with my | tongue:
     I will keep a guard on my mouth * while the | wicked · are | in my | sight.'

2 I held my tongue and | said | nothing:
     I kept | silent · but | found no | comfort.

3 My pain was increased   my heart grew | hot with|in me:
     while I mused the fire blazed and I | spoke | with my | tongue;

4 'Lord let me | know my | end:
     and the | number | of my | days,

† 5 'That I may know how | short my | time is:
     for you have made my days but a handsbreadth *
     and my whole | span · is as | nothing · be|fore you.'

6 Surely every man though he stand secure | is but | breath:
     man | lives · as a | passing | shadow.

7 The riches he heaps are but a | puff of | wind:
     and he cannot | tell | who will | gather them.

8 And now Lord | what is · my | hope?:
     truly my | hope | is in | you.

9 O deliver me from | all · my trans|gressions:
     do not | make me · the | butt of | fools.

10 I was dumb   I did not | open · my | mouth:
     for surely | it was | your | doing.

11 Take away your | plague | from me:
     I am brought to an | end · by the | blows · of your | hand.

12 When with rebukes you chastise a | man for | sin:
     you cause his fair looks to dissolve in putrefaction *
     surely | every · man | is but | breath.

13 Hear my prayer O Lord   and give | ear to · my | cry:
     be not | silent | at my | tears.

14 For I am but a | stranger · with | you:
     a passing guest as | all my | fathers | were.

15 Turn your eye from me   that I may ˈ smile aˈgain:
    before I go ˈ hence and ˈ am no ˈ more.

40

GEORGE J. ELVEY

113

1 I waited patiently ˈ for the ˈ Lord:
   and he inˈclined to me · and ˈ heard my ˈ cry.

2 He brought me up from the pit of roaring waters * out of the ˈ mire and ˈ clay:
   and set my feet upon a ˈ rock · and made ˈ firm my ˈ foothold.

3 And he has put a new ˈ song · in my ˈ mouth:
   even a song of ˈ thanks·giving ˈ to our ˈ God.

4 Many shall ˈ see it · and ˈ fear:
   and shall ˈ put their ˈ trust · in the ˈ Lord.

5 Blessèd is the man who has made the ˈ Lord his ˈ hope:
   who has not turned to the proud * or to those who ˈ wander ˈ in deˈceit.

6 O Lord my God * great are the wonderful things which you have done *
      and your thoughts which ˈ are toˈwards us:
   there is none to ˈ be comˈpared with ˈ you;

† 7 Were I to deˈclare them · and ˈ speak of them:
     they are more than I am ˈ able ˈ to exˈpress.

114   JOHN GOSS from JEREMIAH CLARKE

8 Sacrifice and offering you do ˈ not deˈsire:
   but my ˈ ears · you have ˈ marked · for oˈbedience;

9 Burnt-offering and sin-offering you have ˈ not reˈquired:
   then ˈ said I ˈ Lo I ˈ come.

continued

10 In the scroll of the book it is written of me * that I should ǀ do your ǀ will:
   O my God I long to do it * your ǀ law deǀlights my ǀ heart.

11 I have declared your righteousness in the ǀ great · congreǀgation:
   I have not restrained my lips O ǀ Lord and ǀ that you ǀ know.

12 I have not hidden your righteousness ǀ in my ǀ heart:
   I have spoken of your faithfulness ǀ and of ǀ your salǀvation.

13 I have not kept back your loving-kindness ǀ and your ǀ truth:
   from the ǀ great ǀ congreǀgation.

† 14 O Lord do not withhold your ǀ mercy ǀ from me:
   let your loving-kindness and your ǀ truth ǀ ever · preǀserve me.

15 For innumerable troubles have ǀ come upǀon me:
   my sins have overtaken me ǀ and I ǀ cannot ǀ see.

16 They are more in number than the ǀ hairs · of my ǀ head:
   thereǀfore my ǀ heart ǀ fails me.

17 Be pleased O ǀ Lord · to deǀliver me:
   O ǀ Lord make ǀ haste to ǀ help me.

18 Let those who seek my life to ǀ take it · aǀway:
   be put to shame and conǀfounded ǀ altoǀgether.

19 Let them be turned back and disgraced who ǀ wish me ǀ evil:
   let them be aghast for shame who ǀ say to me · 'Aǀha aǀha!'

20 Let all who seek you be joyful and ǀ glad beǀcause of you:
   let those who love your salvation say ǀ always · 'The ǀ Lord is ǀ great.'

21 As for me I am ǀ poor and ǀ needy:
   but the ǀ Lord will ǀ care ǀ for me.

22 You are my helper and ǀ my deǀliverer:
   make no long deǀlay O ǀ Lord my ǀ God.

41

JAMES TURLE

1 Blessèd is he that considers the ǀ poor and ǀ helpless:
  the Lord will deliver him ǀ in the ǀ day of ǀ trouble.

2 The Lord will guard him and preserve his life *
  he shall be counted ǀ happy · in the ǀ land:
  you will not give him ǀ over · to the ǀ will · of his ǀ enemies.

† 3 And if he lies sick on his bed the ǀ Lord · will susǀtain him:
  if illness lays him ǀ low · you will ǀ overǀthrow it.

4 I said 'O Lord be ǀ merciful · toǀward me:
  heal me for ǀ I have ǀ sinned aǀgainst you.'

5 My enemies speak evil ǀ of me ǀ saying:
  'When will he die and his ǀ name ǀ perish · for ǀ ever?'

6 And if one should come to see me   he mouths ǀ empty ǀ words:
  while his heart gathers mischief * and ǀ when he · goes ǀ out he ǀ vents it.

7 All those that hate me whisper toǀgether · aǀgainst me:
  they deǀvise ǀ plots aǀgainst me.

8 They say   'A deadly ǀ thing has · got ǀ hold of him:
  he will not get up aǀgain from ǀ where he ǀ lies.'

9 Even my bosom friend in ǀ whom I ǀ trusted:
  who shared my bread   has ǀ lifted · his ǀ heel aǀgainst me.

10 But you O Lord be gracious and ǀ raise me ǀ up:
  and I will repay them ǀ what they ǀ have deǀserved.

11 By this will I ǀ know that · you ǀ favour me:
  that my enemy ǀ shall not ǀ triumph ǀ over me.

(†)12 Because of my innocence you ǀ hold me ǀ fast:
  you have set me beǀfore your ǀ face for ǀ ever.

(13 Blessèd be the Lord the ǀ God of ǀ Israel:
  from everlasting to everlasting * ǀ Amen ǀ Aǀmen.)

42

SAMUEL WESLEY

1 As a deer longs for the | running | brooks:
   so longs my | soul for | you O | God.

2 My soul is thirsty for God * thirsty for the | living | God:
   when shall I | come and | see his | face?

3 My tears have been my food | day and | night:
   while they ask me all day long | 'Where now | is your | God?'

4 As I pour out my soul by myself I re|member | this:
   how I went to the house of the Mighty One | into · the | temple · of | God,

† 5 To the shouts and | songs of · thanks|giving:
   a multitude | keeping | high | festival.

6 *Why are you so full of | heaviness · my | soul:*
   and | why · so un|quiet · with|in me?

7 *O put your | trust in | God:*
   *for I will praise him yet * who is my de|liver·er | and my | God.*

8 My soul is | heavy · with|in me:
   therefore I will remember you from the land of Jordan *
      from Mizar a|mong the | hills of | Hermon.

9 Deep calls to deep in the | roar of · your | waters;
   all your waves and | breakers | have gone | over me.

10 Surely the Lord will grant his loving mercy | in the | day-time:
   and in the night his song will be with me * a | prayer · to the | God · of my | life.

11 I will say to God my rock   'Why have | you for|gotten me:
   why must I go like a mourner be|cause the | enemy · op|presses me?'

† 12 Like a sword through my bones my | enemies · have | mocked me:
   while they ask me all day long | 'Where now | is your | God?'

13 *Why are you so full of | heaviness · my | soul:*
   and | why · so un|quiet · with|in me?

14 *O put your | trust in | God:*
   *for I will praise him yet * who is my de|liver·er | and my | God.*

43

SAMUEL WESLEY

1 Give judgement for me O God * take up my cause against an un|godly | people:
  deliver me from de|ceitful · and | wicked | men.

2 For you are God my refuge   why have you | turned · me a|way:
  why must I go like a mourner be|cause the | enemy · op|presses me?

3 O send out your light and your truth and | let them | lead me:
  let them guide me to your holy | hill and | to your | dwelling.

4 Then I shall go to the altar of God * to God my joy and | my de|light:
  and to the harp I shall sing your | praises · O | God my | God.

5 *Why are you so full of* | *heaviness · my* | *soul:*
  and | *why · so un*|*quiet · with*|*in me?*

6 *O put your* | *trust in* | *God:*
  *for I will praise him yet * who is my de*|*liver·er* | *and my* | *God.*

44

ALAN GRAY

1 We have heard with our ears O God our | fathers · have | told us:
  what things you did in their | time · in the | days of | old;

2 How by your own hand you drove out the nations and | planted · us | in:
  how you crushed the peoples * but caused | us to | root and | grow.

3 For it was not by their swords that our fathers took pos|session · of the | land:
  nor did their own | arm | get them · the | victory,

4 But your right hand   your arm and the | light of · your | countenance:
  be|cause · you de|lighted · in | them.

5 You are my | king · and my | God:
  who or|dained | victory · for | Jacob.

6 By your power we struck our | ene·mies | through:
  in your name we trod down | those that | rose a|gainst us.

7 For I did not | trust · in my | bow:
  nor | could my | sword | save me;

8 But it was you that delivered us | from our | enemies:
  and put our | adver·saries | to con|fusion.

† 9 In God we made our boast | all the · day | long:
  we gave | thanks to · your | name with·out | ceasing.

45

FREDERICK A. G. OUSELEY

1 My heart is astir with fine phrases * I make my | song · for a | king:
   my tongue is the | pen · of a | ready | writer.

2 You are the fairest of the sons of men * grace | flows · from your | lips:
   therefore has God | blessed you · for | ever · and | ever.

3 Gird your sword upon your thigh O | mighty | warrior:
   in glory and majesty tread | down your | foes and | triumph!

4 Ride on in the | cause of | truth:
   and | for the | sake of | justice.

5 Your right hand shall teach a | terrible · in|struction:
   peoples shall fall beneath you *
       your arrows shall be sharp in the | hearts · of the | king's | enemies.

6 Your throne is the throne of God   it en|dures for | ever:
   and the sceptre of your | kingdom · is a | righteous | sceptre.

7 You have loved righteousness and | hated | evil:
   therefore God your God *
       has anointed you with the oil of | gladness · a|bove your | fellows.

8 All your garments are fragrant with myrrh | aloes · and | cassia:
   music from ivory | pala·ces | makes you | glad.

† 9 Kings' daughters are among your | noble | women:
   the queen is at your right | hand in | gold of | Ophir.

WILLIAM HAWES

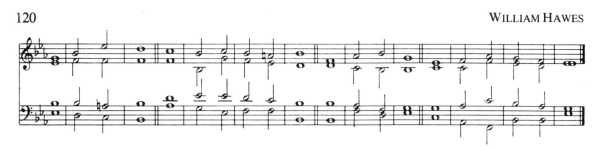

10 Hear O daughter   consider and in|cline your | ear:
    forget your own | people · and your | father's | house.

continued

11 The king de|sires your | beauty:
    he is your lord | therefore · bow | down be|fore him.

† 12 The richest among the people O | daughter · of | Tyre:
    shall en|treat your | favour · with | gifts.

13 The king's daughter is all | glorious · with|in:
    her clothing is em|broidered | cloth of | gold.

14 In robes of many colours she is led to | you O | king:
    and after her the | virgins | that are | with her.

† 15 They are led with | gladness · and re|joicing:
    they enter the | palace | of the | king.

16 In place of your fathers | you shall · have | sons:
    and make them princes | over | all the | land.

17 And I will make known your name to every | gener|ation:
    therefore the peoples shall | give you | praise for | ever.

46

Adapted from LUTHER

1 God is our | refuge · and | strength:
  a very | present | help in | trouble.

2 Therefore we will not fear though the | earth be | moved:
  and though the mountains are | shaken · in the | midst · of the | sea;

† 3 Though the waters | rage and | foam:
  and though the mountains quake at the | rising | of the | sea.

4 There is a river whose streams make glad the | city · of | God:
  the holy dwelling-place | of the | Most | High.

5 God is in the midst of her * therefore she shall | not be | moved:
  God will | help her · and at | break of | day.

6 The nations make uproar and the | kingdoms · are | shaken:
  but God has lifted his | voice · and the | earth shall | tremble.

UNISON
with
Descant
7 *The Lord of | hosts is | with us:*
  the God of | Jacob | is our | stronghold.

8 Come then and see what the | Lord has | done:
  what destruction he has | brought up|on the | earth.

9 He makes wars to cease in | all the | world:
  he breaks the bow and shatters the spear * and burns the | chari·ots | in the | fire.

10 'Be still and know that | I am | God:
  I will be exalted among the nations * I will be ex|alted · up|on the | earth.'

UNISON
with
Descant
11 *The Lord of | hosts is | with us:*
  the God of | Jacob | is our | stronghold.

47

JOHN GOSS

1 O clap your hands ' all you ' peoples:
   and cry aloud to ' God with ' shouts of ' joy.

2 For the Lord Most High ' is to · be ' feared:
   he is a great ' King · over ' all the ' earth.

3 He cast down ' peoples ' under us:
   and the ' nations · be'neath our ' feet.

4 He chose us a land for ' our pos'session:
   that was the pride of ' Jacob ' whom he ' loved.

5 God has gone up with the ' sound · of re'joicing:
   and the ' Lord · to the ' blast · of the ' horn.

6 O sing praises sing ' praises · to ' God:
   O sing praises sing ' praises ' to our ' King.

7 For God is the King of ' all the ' earth:
   O ' praise him · in a ' well-wrought ' psalm.

8 God has become the ' King · of the ' nations:
   he has taken his seat up'on his ' holy ' throne.

9 The princes of the peoples are ' gathered · to'gether:
   with the ' people · of the ' God of ' Abraham.

10 For the mighty ones of the earth are become the ' servants · of ' God:
   and ' he is ' greatly · ex'alted.

48

'TRENT'

1 Great is the Lord and ' greatly · to be ' praised:
    in the ' city ' of our ' God.

2 High and beautiful is his ' holy ' hill:
    it is the ' joy of ' all the ' earth.

† 3 On Mount Zion where godhead truly dwells * stands the city of the ' Great ' King:
    God is well known in her palaces ' as a ' sure de'fence.

4 For the kings of the ' earth as'sembled:
    they gathered to'gether · and ' came ' on;

5 They saw   they were ' struck ' dumb:
    they were a'stonished · and ' fled in ' terror.

6 Trembling took ' hold on them · and ' anguish:
    as on a ' woman ' in her ' travail;

7 Like the breath of the ' east ' wind:
    that ' shatters · the ' ships of ' Tarshish.

8 As we have heard   so have we seen in the city of the ' Lord of ' hosts:
    in the city of our God which ' God · has es'tablished · for ' ever.

9 We have called to mind your loving-'kindness · O ' God:
    in the ' midst of ' your ' temple.

10 As your name is great O God   so also ' is your ' praise:
    even to the ' ends ' of the ' earth.

11 Your right hand is full of victory * let Zion's ' hill re'joice:
    let the daughters of Judah be ' glad be'cause of · your ' judgements.

12 Walk about Zion   go round about her and ' count · all her ' towers:
    consider well her ramparts ' pass ' through her ' palaces;

13 That you may tell those who come after that ' such is ' God:
    our God for ever and ever * and ' he will ' guide us · e'ternally.

49

THOMAS A. WALMISLEY

1 O hear this | all you | peoples:
    give ear all you in|habit·ants | of the | world,

2 All children of men and | sons of | Adam:
    both | rich and | poor a|like.

3 For my mouth shall | speak | wisdom:
    and the thoughts of my heart shall be | full of | under|standing.

4 I will incline my | ear · to a | riddle:
    and unfold the mystery to the | sounds | of the | harp.

5 Why should I fear in the | evil | days:
    when the wickedness of | my de|ceivers · sur|rounds me,

6 Though they trust to their | great | wealth:
    and boast of the a|bundance | of their | riches?

7 No man may | ransom · his | brother:
    or give | God a | price | for him,

8 So that he may | live for | ever:
    and | never | see the | grave;

9 For to ransom men's | lives · is so | costly:
    that he must a|bandon | it for | ever.

10 For we see that | wise men | die:
    and perish with the foolish and the ignorant * | leaving · their | wealth to | others.

11 The tomb is their home for ever * their dwelling-place throughout | all · gener|ations:
    though they called estates | after · their | own | names.

12 A rich man without | under|standing:
    is | like the | beasts that | perish.

13 This is the | lot · of the | foolish:
    the end of those who are | pleased · with their | own | words.

14 They are driven like sheep into the grave and | death · is their | shepherd:
    they slip down | easi·ly | into · the | tomb.

15 Their bright forms shall wear a|way · in the | grave:
    and | lose their | former | glory.

16 But God will | ransom · my | life:
    he will take me | from the | power · of the | grave.

50

WILLIAM BOYCE

1 The Lord our God the | Mighty One · has | spoken:
  and summoned the earth * from the rising of the sun to its | setting | in the | west.

2 From Zion | perfect · in | beauty:
  God has | shone | out in | glory.

3 Our God is coming   he will | not keep | silent:
  before him is devouring fire * and | tempest | whirls a|bout him.

4 He calls to the | heavens · a|bove:
  and to the earth so | he may | judge his | people.

5 'Gather to | me my | faithful ones:
  those who by sacrifice | made a | coven·ant | with me.'

6 The heavens shall pro|claim his | righteousness:
  for | God him|self is | judge.

7 'Listen my people and | I will | speak:
  O Israel I am God your God   and | I will | give my | testimony.

8 'It is not for your sacrifices that | I re|prove you:
  for your burnt-|offerings · are | always · be|fore me.

9 'I will take no | bull · from your | farms:
  or | he-goat | from your | pens.

10 'For all the beasts of the forest be|long to | me:
  and so do the | cattle · up|on the | mountains.

11 'I know all the | birds · of the | air:
  and the grasshoppers of the | field are | in my | sight.

12 'If I were hungry I | would not | tell you:
  for the whole world is | mine and | all · that is | in it.

13 'Do I eat the | flesh of | bulis:
  or | drink the | blood of | goats?

14 'Offer to God a sacrifice of | thanks|giving:
  and pay your | vows · to the | Most | High.

† 15 'Call upon me in the | day of | trouble:
  I will bring you out   and | you shall | glori·fy | me.'

continued

HENRY T. SMART

16 But God ˈ says · to the ˈ wicked:
   'What have you to do with reciting my laws *
   or taking my ˈ coven·ant ˈ on your ˈ lips,

17 'Seeing you ˈ loathe ˈ discipline:
   and have ˈ tossed my ˈ words beˈhind you?

18 'When you saw a thief you ˈ went aˈlong with him:
   and you ˈ threw in · your ˈ lot · with adˈulterers.

19 'You have loosed your ˈ mouth in ˈ evil:
   and your ˈ tongue strings ˈ lies toˈgether.

20 'You sit and speak aˈgainst your ˈ brother:
   and slander your ˈ own ˈ mother's ˈ son.

21 'These things you have done   and I ˈ held my ˈ tongue:
   and you thought I was just such anˈother ˈ as yourˈself.

22 'But I ˈ will conˈvict you:
   and set before your ˈ eyes what ˈ you have ˈ done.

23 'O consider this   you who forˈget ˈ God:
   lest I tear you in pieces   and ˈ there be ˈ no one · to ˈ save you.

† 24 'He honours me who brings sacrifice of ˈ thanksˈgiving:
   and to him who keeps to my way I will ˈ show the · salˈvation · of ˈ God.

51

JOHN STAINER

1 Have mercy on me O God in your enˈduring ˈ goodness:
   according to the fulness of your compassion ˈ blot out ˈ my ofˈfences.

2 Wash me thoroughly | from my | wickedness:
and | cleanse me | from my | sin.

3 For I acknowledge | my re|bellion:
and my | sin is | ever · be|fore me.

4 Against you only have I sinned * and done what is evil | in your | eyes:
so you will be just in your sentence * and | blameless | in your | judging.

5 Surely in wickedness I was | brought to | birth:
and in | sin my | mother · con|ceived me.

6 You that desire truth in the | inward | parts:
O teach me wisdom in the secret | places | of the | heart.

7 Purge me with hyssop and I | shall be | clean:
wash me and I | shall be | whiter · than | snow.

8 Make me hear of | joy and | gladness:
let the bones which | you have | broken · re|joice.

9 Hide your | face · from my | sins:
and | blot out | all · my in|iquities.

10 Create in me a clean | heart O | God:
and re|new a · right | spirit · with|in me.

11 Do not cast me | out · from your | presence:
do not take your | holy | spirit | from me.

12 O give me the gladness of your | help a|gain:
and sup|port me · with a | willing | spirit.

† 13 Then will I teach trans|gressors · your | ways:
and sinners shall | turn to | you a|gain.

14 O Lord God of my salvation de|liver me · from | bloodshed:
and my | tongue shall | sing of · your | righteousness.

15 O Lord | open · my | lips:
and my | mouth · shall pro|claim your | praise.

16 You take no pleasure in sacrifice or | I would | give it:
burnt-|offerings · you | do not | want.

17 The sacrifice of God is a | broken | spirit:
a broken and contrite heart O God | you will | not de|spise.

18 In your graciousness do | good to | Zion:
re|build the | walls · of Je|rusalem.

19 Then will you delight in right sacrifices * in burnt-offerings | and ob|lations:
then will they offer young | bulls up|on your | altar.

54

JAMES NARES

1 Save me O God by the | power of · your | name:
   and | vindicate · me | by your | might.

2 Hear my | prayer O | God:
   and | listen · to the | words of · my | mouth.

3 For the insolent have | risen · a|gainst me:
   ruthless men who have not set God be|fore them | seek my | life.

4 But surely | God is · my | helper:
   the Lord is the up|holder | of my | life.

[5 Let evil recoil on those that | would way|lay me:
   O de|stroy them | in your | faithfulness!]

6 Then will I offer you sacrifice with a | willing | heart:
   I will praise your name O | Lord for | it is | good.

7 For you will deliver me from | every | trouble:
   my eyes shall see the | downfall | of my | enemies.

55

W. Bayley

1 Hear my | prayer O | God:
  and do not hide your|self from | my pe|tition.

2 Give heed to | me and | answer me:
  I am | restless · in | my com|plaining.

3 I am in turmoil at the | voice · of the | enemy:
  at the | onslaught | of the | wicked.

4 For they bring down dis|aster · up|on me:
  they persecute | me with | bitter | fury.

5 My heart | writhes with|in me:
  and the terrors of | death have | fallen · up|on me.

6 Fear and trembling | come up|on me:
  and | horror | over|whelms me.

7 And I said   'O for the | wings · of a | dove:
  that I might fly a|way and | find | rest.

8 'Then I would | flee far | off:
  and make my | lodging | in the | wilderness.

9 'I would hasten to | find me · a | refuge:
  out | of the | blast of | slander,

10 'Out of the tempest of their | calumny · O | Lord:
  and | far · from their | double | tongues.'

11 For I have seen violence and | strife · in the | city:
  day and night they go | round it · up|on its | walls.

12 Evil and wickedness | are with|in it:
  iniquity is within it * oppression and fraud do | not de|part · from | its streets.

13 It was not an enemy that reviled me * or I | might have | borne it:
  it was not my foe that dealt so insolently with me *
  or I might have | hidden · my|self | from him;

14 But it was you a | man · like my|self:
  my companion | and · my fam|iliar | friend.

† 15 Together we en|joyed sweet | fellowship:
  in the | house | of our | God.

continued

[16 Let them pass a|way · in con|fusion:
    let death | carry · them | to des|truction;

17 Let them go down a|live to | Sheol:
    for evil is a|mong them | in their | dwellings.]

130

18 But I will | call to | God:
    and the | Lord my | God will | save me.

19 At evening at morning | and at | noon-day:
    I com|plain and | groan a|loud.

20 And he will | hear my | voice:
    and | ransom · my | soul in | peace,

21 From those that bear | down up|on me:
    for | there are | many · a|gainst me.

22 God will hear and | bring them | low:
    he that | is en|throned for | ever.

23 For they do not | keep their | word:
    and they | have no | fear of | God.

24 They lay violent hands on those that | are at | peace with them:
    they | break | solemn | covenants.

25 Their mouths are smooth as butter * but war is | in their | hearts:
    their words are softer than oil * yet | they are | drawn | swords.

26 Cast your burden on the Lord and | he · will sus|tain you:
    he will never suffer the | righteous | man to | stumble.

27 But as for them   you will bring them | down O | God:
    even | to the | depths · of the | Pit.

† 28 Bloodthirsty and deceitful men shall not live out | half their | days:
    but | I will | trust in | you.

56

GEORGE COOPER

1   Be merciful to me O God   for men are ˈ treading · me ˈ down:
    all day long my ˈ adver·sary ˈ presses · upˈon me.

2   My enemies tread me down ˈ all the ˈ day:
    for there are many that ˈ arrogant·ly ˈ fight aˈgainst me.

3   In the ˈ hour of ˈ fear:
    I will ˈ put my ˈ trust in ˈ you.

4   In God whose word I praise * in God I ˈ trust and ˈ fear not:
    what can ˈ flesh ˈ do to ˈ me?

5   All day long they afflict me ˈ with their ˈ words:
    and every thought is ˈ how to ˈ do me ˈ evil.

6   They stir up hatred ˈ and conˈceal themselves:
    they watch my steps   while they ˈ lie in ˈ wait for · my ˈ life.

7   Let there be ˈ no esˈcape for them:
    bring down the ˈ peoples · in your ˈ wrath O ˈ God.

8   You have counted my anxious tossings * put my ˈ tears · in your ˈ bottle:
    are not these things ˈ noted ˈ in your ˈ book?

9   In the day that I call to you   my enemies shall ˈ turn ˈ back:
    this I ˈ know for ˈ God is ˈ with me.

10 In God whose word I praise * in God I ˈ trust and ˈ fear not:
    what can ˈ man ˈ do to ˈ me?

11 To you O God must I perˈform my ˈ vows:
    I will pay the thank-ˈoffer·ing ˈ that is ˈ due.

12 For you will deliver my soul from death and my ˈ feet from ˈ falling:
    that I may walk before ˈ God · in the ˈ light · of the ˈ living.

57

EDWARD J. HOPKINS

1 Be merciful to me O ˈ God be ˈ merciful:
   for I ˈ come to ˈ you for ˈ shelter;

2 And in the shadow of your wings will ˈ I take ˈ refuge:
   until these ˈ troubles · are ˈ over-ˈpast.

3 I will call to ˈ God Most ˈ High:
   to the God who will fulˈfil his ˈ purpose ˈ for me.

4 He will send from ˈ heaven · and ˈ save me:
   he will send forth his faithfulness and his loving-kindness *
      and rebuke ˈ those · that would ˈ trample · me ˈ down.

5 For I lie amidst ˈ raven·ing ˈ lions:
   men whose teeth are spears and arrows *
      and their ˈ tongue a ˈ sharpened ˈ sword.

UNISON 6 *Be exalted O God aˈbove the ˈ heavens:*
   and let your glory be ˈ over ˈ all the ˈ earth.

7 They have set a net for my feet   and I am ˈ brought ˈ low:
   they have dug a pit before me * but shall ˈ fall · into ˈ it themˈselves.

8 My heart is fixed O God my ˈ heart is ˈ fixed:
   I will ˈ sing and ˈ make ˈ melody.

9 Awake my soul   awake ˈ lute and ˈ harp:
   for ˈ I · will aˈwaken · the ˈ morning.

10 I will give you thanks O Lord aˈmong the ˈ peoples:
   I will sing your ˈ praise aˈmong the ˈ nations.

11 For the greatness of your mercy ˈ reaches · to the ˈ heavens:
   and your ˈ faithful·ness ˈ to the ˈ clouds.

UNISON 12 *Be exalted O God aˈbove the ˈ heavens:*
   and let your glory be ˈ over ˈ all the ˈ earth.

59

133

W. G. ALCOCK

1 Deliver me from my ˈ enemies · O ˈ God:
　 lift me to safety from ˈ those that ˈ rise aˈgainst me;

2 O deliver me from the ˈ evilˈdoers:
　 and ˈ save me · from ˈ blood·thirsty ˈ men.

3 For they lie in ˈ wait · for my ˈ life:
　 savage men ˈ stir up ˈ violence · aˈgainst me.

4 Not for my sin or my transgression O Lord * not for any ˈ evil · I have ˈ done:
　 do they run and take ˈ up poˈsition · aˈgainst me.

(†)5 Arise to ˈ meet me · and ˈ see:
　 you that are Lord of ˈ hosts and ˈ God of ˈ Israel.

[6 Awake to punish ˈ all the ˈ nations:
　 have no mercy on those that so ˈ treacherous·ly ˈ do ˈ wrong.]

7 They return every evening　they ˈ howl like ˈ dogs:
　 they ˈ prowl aˈround the ˈ city.

8 Look how their ˈ mouths ˈ slaver:
　 swords strike from their lips * for they ˈ say ˈ 'Who will ˈ hear it?"

9 But you O Lord will ˈ laugh them · to ˈ scorn:
　 you will deˈride ˈ all the ˈ nations.

10 I will look to ˈ you · O my ˈ strength:
　 for ˈ God is · my ˈ strong ˈ tower.

11 My God in his steadfastness will ˈ come to ˈ meet me:
　 God will show me the ˈ downfall ˈ of my ˈ enemies.

12 Slay them not O Lord　lest my ˈ people · forˈget:
　 but make them stagger by your ˈ power and ˈ bring them ˈ down.

13 Give them over to punishment *
　　 for the sin of their mouths for the ˈ words of · their ˈ lips:
　 let them be ˈ taken ˈ in their ˈ pride.

[14 For the curses and lies that they have uttered * O consume them ˈ in your ˈ wrath:
　 consume them·ˈ till they ˈ are no ˈ more;]

[†]15 That men may know that God ˈ rules · over ˈ Jacob:
　 even to the ˈ ends ˈ of the ˈ earth.

continued

95

16 They return every evening   they | howl like | dogs:
    they | prowl a|round the | city.

17 They roam here and there | looking · for | food:
    and | growl · if they | are not | filled.

18 But I will | sing of · your | might:
    I will sing aloud each | morning | of your | goodness.

19 For you have been my | strong | tower:
    and a sure refuge in the | day of | my dis|tress.

† 20 I will sing your praises | O my | strength:
    for | God is · my | strong | tower.

60

1 O God you have cast us | off and | broken us:
   you were enraged against us | O re|store us · a|gain!

2 You have caused the land to quake   you have | rent it | open:
   heal the rifts for the | earth | quivers · and | breaks.

3 You have steeped your people in a | bitter | draught:
   you have given them a | wine to | make them | stagger.

4 You have caused those that fear you to | take | flight:
   so that they | run | from the | bow.

† 5 O save us by your right | hand and | answer us:
   that those whom you | love may | be de|livered.

6   God has said in his | holy | place:
     'I will exult and divide Shechem * I will parcel | out the | valley · of | Succoth.

7   'Gilead is mine and Ma|nasseh · is | mine:
     Ephraim is my helmet and | Judah · my | rod · of com|mand.

† 8   'Moab is my wash-bowl   over Edom will I | cast my | shoe:
     against Philistia | will I | shout in | triumph.'

9   Who will lead me into the | forti·fied | city:
     who will | bring me | into | Edom?

10   Have you not cast us | off O | God?:
     you | go not | out · with our | armies.

11   Give us your help a|gainst the | enemy:
     for | vain · is the | help of | man.

12   By the power of our God we | shall do | valiantly:
     for it is he that will | tread | down our | enemies.

61

135

CHARLES H. LLOYD

1   Hear my loud | crying · O | God:
     and give | heed | to my | prayer.

2   From the ends of the earth I call to you when my | heart | faints:
     O set me on the | rock · that is | higher · than | I.

3   For you have | been my | refuge:
     and my strong | tower a|gainst the | enemy.

4   I will dwell in your | tent for | ever:
     and find shelter in the | cover·ing | of your | wings.

5   For you have heard my | vows O | God:
     you have granted the desire of | those that | fear your | name.

6   You will give the | king long | life:
     and his years shall endure through | many | gener|ations.

7   He shall dwell before | God for | ever:
     loving-kindness and | truth shall | be his | guard.

8   So will I ever sing praises | to your | name:
     while I | daily · per|form my | vows.

62

WILLIAM BOYCE

1 My soul waits in ˈ silence · for ˈ God:
   for from ˈ him comes ˈ my salˈvation.

2 He only is my rock and ˈ my salˈvation:
   my strong tower   so that ˈ I shall ˈ never · be ˈ moved.

3 How long will you all plot against a ˈ man · to deˈstroy him:
   as though he were a leaning ˈ fence · or a ˈ buckling ˈ wall?

4 Their design is to thrust him from his height * and their deˈlight · is in ˈ lies:
   they bless with their ˈ lips but ˈ inwardly · they ˈ curse.

5 Nevertheless my soul   wait in ˈ silence · for ˈ God:
   for from ˈ him ˈ comes my ˈ hope.

6 He only is my rock and ˈ my salˈvation:
   my strong tower   so that ˈ I shall ˈ not be ˈ moved.

7 In God is my deliverance ˈ and my ˈ glory:
   God is my strong ˈ rock ˈ and my ˈ shelter.

8 Trust in him at all times ˈ O my ˈ people:
   pour out your hearts before him   for ˈ God ˈ is our ˈ refuge.

9 The children of men are but breath * the children of ˈ men · are a ˈ lie:
   place them in the scales and they fly upward * they ˈ are as ˈ light as ˈ air.

10 Put no trust in extortion * do not grow ˈ worthless · by ˈ robbery:
   if riches increase ˈ set not · your ˈ heart upˈon them.

11 God has spoken once   twice have I ˈ heard him ˈ say:
   that ˈ power beˈlongs to ˈ God,

12 That to the Lord belongs a ˈ constant ˈ goodness:
   for you reward a man acˈcording ˈ to his ˈ works.

63

WALTER PARRATT

1 O God ˈ you are · my ˈ God:
  eagerly ˈ will I ˈ seek ˈ you.

2 My soul thirsts for you   my ˈ flesh ˈ longs for you:
  as a dry and thirsty ˈ land · where no ˈ water ˈ is.

3 So it was when I beheld you ˈ in the ˈ sanctuary:
  and ˈ saw your ˈ power · and your ˈ glory.

4 For your unchanging goodness is ˈ better · than ˈ life:
  thereˈfore my ˈ lips shall ˈ praise you.

5 And so I will bless you as ˈ long as · I ˈ live:
  and in your name will I ˈ lift my ˈ hands on ˈ high.

6 My longing shall be satisfied as with ˈ marrow · and ˈ fatness:
  my mouth shall ˈ praise you · with exˈultant ˈ lips.

7 When I remember you upˈon my ˈ bed:
  when I meditate upˈon you · in the ˈ night ˈ watches,

8 How you have ˈ been my ˈ helper:
  then I sing for joy in the ˈ shadow ˈ of your ˈ wings,

† 9 Then my ˈ soul ˈ clings to you:
  and ˈ your right ˈ hand upˈholds me.

65

GEORGE M. GARRETT

(small notes for organ only)

1 You are to be praised O ˈ God in ˈ Zion:
   to you shall vows be paid ˈ you that ˈ answer ˈ prayer.

2 To you shall all flesh come to conˈfess their ˈ sins:
   when our misdeeds prevail against us ˈ you will ˈ purge · them aˈway.

† 3 Blessèd is the man you choose *
   and take to yourself to dwell withˈin your ˈ courts:
   we shall be filled with the good things of your house   ˈ of your ˈ holy ˈ temple.

4 You will answer us in your righteousness with terrible deeds O ˈ God our ˈ saviour:
   you that are the hope of all the ends of the earth and ˈ of the ˈ distant ˈ seas;

5 Who by your strength made ˈ fast the ˈ mountains:
   you ˈ that are ˈ girded · with ˈ power;

6 Who stilled the raging of the seas the ˈ roaring · of the ˈ waves:
   and the ˈ tumult ˈ of the ˈ peoples.

7 Those who dwell at the ends of the earth are aˈfraid at · your ˈ wonders:
   the dawn and the ˈ even·ing ˈ sing your ˈ praises.

8 You tend the ˈ earth and ˈ water it:
   you ˈ make it ˈ rich and ˈ fertile.

9 The river of God is ˈ full of ˈ water:
   and so providing for the earth you proˈvide ˈ grain for ˈ men.

10 You drench its furrows   you level the ˈ ridges · beˈtween:
   you soften it with showers and ˈ bless its ˈ early ˈ growth.

11 You crown the ˈ year · with your ˈ goodness:
   and the tracks where you have ˈ passed ˈ drip with ˈ fatness.

12 The pastures of the ˈ wilderness · run ˈ over:
   and the ˈ hills are ˈ girded · with ˈ joy.

13 The meadows are ˈ clothed with ˈ sheep:
   and the valleys stand so thick with corn they ˈ shout for ˈ joy and ˈ sing.

66

GEORGE J. ELVEY

1 O shout with joy to God ¦ all the ¦ earth:
 sing to the honour of his name * and give him ¦ glory ¦ as his ¦ praise.

2 Say to God 'How fearful ¦ are your ¦ works:
 because of your great might your ¦ enemies · shall ¦ cower · be¦fore you.'

3 All the ¦ earth shall ¦ worship you:
 and sing to you   and sing ¦ praises ¦ to your ¦ name.

4 Come then and see what ¦ God has ¦ done:
 how terrible are his ¦ dealings · with the ¦ children · of ¦ men.

5 He turned the sea into dry land * they crossed the ¦ river · on ¦ foot:
 then ¦ were we ¦ joyful · be¦cause of him.

6 By his power he rules for ever * his eyes keep ¦ watch · on the ¦ nations:
 and rebels shall ¦ never ¦ rise a¦gainst him.

7 O bless our ¦ God you ¦ peoples:
 and cause his ¦ praises ¦ to re¦sound,

8 Who has held our ¦ souls in ¦ life:
 who has not ¦ suffered · our ¦ feet to ¦ slip.

9 For you have ¦ proved us · O ¦ God:
 you have ¦ tried us · as ¦ silver · is ¦ tried.

10 You brought us ¦ into · the ¦ net:
 you laid sharp ¦ torment ¦ on our ¦ loins.

† 11 You let men ride over our heads * we went through ¦ fire and ¦ water:
 but you brought us out ¦ into · a ¦ place of ¦ liberty.

12 I will come into your house with ¦ burnt-¦offerings:
 and ¦ I will ¦ pay you · my ¦ vows,

13 The vows that ¦ opened · my ¦ lips:
 that my mouth uttered ¦ when I ¦ was in ¦ trouble.

14 I will offer you burnt-offerings of fattened beasts * with the sweet ¦ smoke of ¦ rams:
 I will sacrifice a ¦ bull · and the ¦ flesh of ¦ goats.

15 Come then and hear   all ¦ you that · fear ¦ God:
 and I will ¦ tell what ¦ he has ¦ done for me.

continued

GEORGE J. ELVEY

16 I called to him ǀ with my ǀ mouth:
and his ǀ praise was ǀ on my ǀ tongue.

17 If I had cherished wickedness ǀ in my ǀ heart:
the ǀ Lord would ǀ not have ǀ heard me.

18 But ǀ God has ǀ heard me:
he has ǀ heeded · the ǀ voice of · my ǀ prayer.

19 Praise ǀ be to ǀ God:
who has not turned back my prayer * or his ǀ steadfast ǀ love ǀ from me.

67

JAMES NARES

1 Let God be gracious to ǀ us and ǀ bless us:
and make his ǀ face ǀ shine upǀon us,

2 That your ways may be ǀ known on ǀ earth:
your liberating ǀ power · aǀmong all ǀ nations.

UNISON
with Descant
3 Let the peoples ǀ praise you · O ǀ God:
let ǀ all the ǀ peoples ǀ praise you.

4 Let the nations be ǀ glad and ǀ sing:
for you judge the peoples with integrity *
and govern the ǀ nations · upǀon ǀ earth.

UNISON
with Descant
5 Let the peoples ǀ praise you · O ǀ God:
let ǀ all the ǀ peoples ǀ praise you.

6 Then the earth will ǀ yield its ǀ fruitfulness:
and ǀ God our ǀ God will ǀ bless us.

7 God ǀ shall ǀ bless us:
and all the ǀ ends · of the ǀ earth will ǀ fear him.

68

JOHN GOSS

1 God shall arise   and his enemies ˈ shall be ˈ scattered:
   those that hate him shall ˈ flee beˈfore his ˈ face.

2 As smoke is dispersed   so shall ˈ they · be disˈpersed:
   as wax melts before a fire * so shall the wicked ˈ perish · at the ˈ presence · of ˈ God.

3 But the righteous shall be glad and exˈult be·fore ˈ God:
   they ˈ shall reˈjoice with ˈ gladness.

4 O sing to God   sing praises ˈ to his ˈ name:
   glorify him that rode through the deserts *
   him whose name is the Lord ˈ and exˈult beˈfore him.

5 He is the father of the fatherless * he upholds the ˈ cause · of the ˈ widow:
   God ˈ in his ˈ holy ˈ dwelling place.

6 He gives the desolate a home to dwell in *
   and brings the prisoners out ˈ into · prosˈperity:
   but rebels must ˈ dwell · in a ˈ barren ˈ land.

7 O God   when you went out beˈfore your ˈ people:
   when you ˈ marched ˈ through the ˈ wilderness,

8 The earth shook   the heavens ˈ poured down ˈ water:
   before the God of Sinai   before ˈ God the ˈ God of ˈ Israel.

9 You showered down a generous ˈ rain O ˈ God:
   you prepared the land of your posˈsession · when ˈ it was ˈ weary.

10 And there your ˈ people ˈ settled:
   in the place that your goodness O God had made ˈ ready ˈ for the ˈ poor.

11 The Lord spoke the word *
   and great was the company of those that ˈ carried · the ˈ tidings:
   'Kings with their armies are ˈ fleeing · are ˈ fleeing · aˈway.

12 'Even the women at home may ˈ share · in the ˈ spoil:
   and will you sit ˈ idly · aˈmong the ˈ sheepfolds?

13 'There are images of doves whose wings are ˈ covered · with ˈ silver:
   and their ˈ pinions · with ˈ shining ˈ gold.'

14 When the Almighty ˈ scattered ˈ kings:
   they were like snow ˈ falling · upˈon Mount ˈ Zalmon.

continued

JOHN GOSS

15 The mountain of Bashan is a ǀ mighty ǀ mountain:
the mountain of Bashan is a ǀ mountain · of ǀ many ǀ peaks.

16 O mountains of many peaks   why ǀ look so ǀ enviously:
at the mountain where God is pleased to dwell *
where the ǀ Lord · will reǀmain for ǀ ever?

17 The chariots of God are twice ten thousand and ǀ thousands up·on ǀ thousands:
the Lord came from Sinai ǀ into · his ǀ holy ǀ place.

18 When you ascended the heights you led the enemy captive *
you received ǀ tribute · from ǀ men:
but rebels shall not ǀ dwell · in the ǀ presence · of ǀ God.

19 Blessèd be the Lord day by day * who bears us ǀ as his ǀ burden:
he is the ǀ God of ǀ our deǀliverance.

20 God is to us a ǀ God who ǀ saves:
by God the Lord do ǀ we esǀcape ǀ death.

69

ROSS

1 Save ǀ me O ǀ God:
for the waters have come up ǀ even ǀ to my ǀ throat.

2 I sink in the deep mire ǀ where no ǀ footing is:
I have come into deep waters ǀ and the ǀ flood sweeps ǀ over me.

3 I am weary with crying out   my ǀ throat is ǀ parched:
my eyes fail with ǀ watching · so ǀ long · for my ǀ God.

4 Those that hate me without cause * are more in number than the ǀ hairs · of my ǀ head:
those that would destroy me are many * they oppose me wrongfully *
for I must restore ǀ things · that I ǀ never ǀ took.

5   O God you [|] know my [|] foolishness:
     and my [|] sins · are not [|] hidden [|] from you.

6   Let not those who wait for you be shamed because of me * O Lord [|] God of [|] hosts:
     let not those who seek you be disgraced on [|] my account · O [|] God of [|] Israel.

7   For your sake have I [|] suffered · re[|]proach:
     and [|] shame has [|] covered · my [|] face.

8   I have become a stranger [|] to my [|] brothers:
     an alien [|] to my · own [|] mother's [|] sons.

9   Zeal for your house has [|] eaten · me [|] up:
     and the taunts of those who taunt [|] you have [|] fallen · on [|] me.

10 I afflicted my[|]self with [|] fasting:
     and that was [|] turned to [|] my re[|]proach.

11 I made [|] sackcloth · my [|] clothing:
     and I be[|]came a [|] byword [|] to them.

12 Those who sit in the gate [|] talk of [|] me:
     and the [|] drunkards · make [|] songs a[|]bout me.

143   ARTHUR H. MANN

13 But to you Lord I [|] make my [|] prayer:
     at [|] an ac[|]cepta·ble [|] time.

14 Answer me O God in your a[|]bundant [|] goodness:
     and [|] with your [|] sure de[|]liverance.

15 Bring me out of the mire   so that I [|] may not [|] sink:
     let me be delivered from my enemies and [|] from the [|] deep [|] waters.

16 Let not the flood overwhelm me * or the depths [|] swallow · me [|] up:
     let not the [|] Pit · shut its [|] mouth up[|]on me.

17 Hear me O Lord   as your loving-[|]kindness · is [|] good:
     turn to me   as [|] your com[|]passion · is [|] great.

18 Do not hide your [|] face · from your [|] servant:
     for I am in trouble   [|] O be [|] swift to [|] answer me!

19 Draw near to me [|] and re[|]deem me:
     O [|] ransom me · be[|]cause of · my [|] enemies!

20 You know [|] all their [|] taunts:
     my adversaries are [|] all [|] in your [|] sight.   *continued*

ARTHUR H. MANN

21 Insults have | broken · my | heart:
    my shame and dis|grace are | past | healing.

22 I looked for someone to have pity on me * but | there was | no man:
    for some to | comfort me · but | found | none.

† 23 They gave me | poison · for | food:
    and when I was thirsty they | gave me | vinegar · to | drink.

71

WILLIAM RUSSELL

1 To you Lord have I | come for | shelter:
    let me | never · be | put to | shame.

2 In your righteousness rescue | and de|liver me:
    incline your | ear to | me and | save me.

3 Be for me a rock of refuge * a fortress | to de|fend me:
    for you are my high | rock | and my | stronghold.

4 Rescue me O my God from the | hand · of the | wicked:
    from the grasp of the | piti·less | and un|just.

5 For you Lord | are my | hope:
    you are my confidence O | God · from my | youth | upward.

6 On you have I | leaned · since my | birth:
    you are he that brought me out of my mother's womb *
      and my | praise · is of | you con|tinually.

7 I have become as a fearful | warning · to | many:
    but | you are · my | strength · and my | refuge.

8 My mouth shall be | filled · with your | praises:
    I shall sing of your | glory | all the · day | long.

WILLIAM RUSSELL

9   Cast me not away in the ǀ time of · old ǀ age:
      nor forsake me ǀ when my ǀ strength ǀ fails.

10 For my enemies ǀ speak aǀgainst me:
      and those that watch for my life conǀspire toǀgether ǀ saying,

† 11 'God ǀ has forǀsaken him:
      pursue him   take him   for ǀ there is ǀ none to ǀ save him.'

12 Be not far ǀ from me · O ǀ God:
      my ǀ God make ǀ haste to ǀ help me.

13 Let my adversaries be confounded and ǀ put to ǀ shame:
      let those who seek my hurt be ǀ covered · with ǀ scorn · and disǀgrace.

14 As for me   I will wait in ǀ hope conǀtinually:
      and I will ǀ praise you ǀ more and ǀ more.

15 My mouth shall speak of your righteousness ǀ all the ǀ day:
      and tell of your salvation ǀ though it · exǀceeds my ǀ telling.

16 I will begin with the mighty acts of the ǀ Lord my ǀ God:
      and declare your righteous ǀ dealing   ǀ yours aǀlone.

17 O God you have taught me from my ǀ youth ǀ upward:
      and to this day I proǀclaim your ǀ marvel·lous ǀ works.

18 Forsake me not O God in my old age   when I am ǀ grey-ǀheaded:
      till I have shown the strength of your arm to future generations *
      and your ǀ might to ǀ those that · come ǀ after.

19 Your righteousness O God ǀ reaches · to the ǀ heavens:
      great are the things that you have done * O ǀ God ǀ who is ǀ like you?

20 You have burdened me with many and bitter troubles * O ǀ turn · and reǀnew me:
      and raise me up aǀgain · from the ǀ depths · of the ǀ earth.

21 Bless me beyond my ǀ former ǀ greatness:
      O ǀ turn to me · aǀgain and ǀ comfort me.

22 Then will I praise you upon the lute for your faithfulness ǀ O my ǀ God:
      and sing your praises to the harp O ǀ Holy ǀ One of ǀ Israel.

23 My lips shall reǀjoice in · my ǀ singing:
      and my soul ǀ also · for ǀ you have ǀ ransomed me.

† 24 My tongue shall speak of your righteous dealing ǀ all the · day ǀ long:
      for they shall be put to shame and disgraced that ǀ seek to ǀ do me ǀ evil.

THOMAS NORRIS

1 Give the king your | judgement · O | God:
  and your righteousness to the | son | of a | king,

2 That he may judge your | people | rightly:
  and the | poor · of the | land with | equity.

3 Let the mountains be laden with peace be|cause of · his | righteousness:
  and the hills also with pros|peri·ty | for his | people.

4 May he give justice to the poor a|mong the | people:
  and rescue the children of the | needy · and | crush · the op|pressor.

5 May he live while the | sun en|dures:
  and while the moon gives light through|out all | gener|ations.

6 May he come down like rain upon the | new-mown | fields:
  and as | showers · that | water · the | earth.

7 In his time shall | righteous·ness | flourish:
  and abundance of peace till the | moon shall | be no | more.

8 His dominion shall stretch from | sea to | sea:
  from the Great | River · to the | ends · of the | earth.

9 His adversaries shall bow | down be|fore him:
  and his | enemies · shall | lick the | dust:

10 The kings of Tarshish and of the isles shall | bring | tribute:
  the kings of Sheba and | Seba · shall | offer | gifts.

† 11 All kings shall fall | down be|fore him:
  and all | nations | do him | service.

12 He will deliver the needy | when they | cry:
  and the | poor man · that | has no | helper.

13 He will pity the helpless | and the | needy:
  and | save the | lives · of the | poor.

† 14 He will redeem them from op|pression · and | violence:
  and their blood shall be | precious | in his | sight.

15 Long may he live   and be given of the | gold of | Sheba:
  may prayer be made for him continually * and men | bless him | every | day.

THOMAS NORRIS

16 Let there be abundance of | wheat · in the | land:
   let it | flourish · on the | tops · of the | mountains;

† 17 Let its ears grow fat like the | grain of | Lebanon:
   and its sheaves | thicken · like the | grass · of the | field.

18 Let his name | live for | ever:
   and en|dure as | long · as the | sun.

19 Let all peoples use his | name in | blessing:
   and all | nations | call him | blessèd.

(20 Blessèd be the Lord God the | God of | Israel:
   who a|lone does | great | wonders.

21 Blessèd be his glorious | name for | ever:
   and let the whole earth be filled with his glory | Amen | A|men.)

73

JOHN SOAPER

1 God is indeed | good to | Israel:
  to | those whose | hearts are | pure.

2 Nevertheless my feet were | almost | gone:
  my | steps had | well-nigh | slipped.

3 For I was filled with envy | at the | boastful:
  when I saw the un|godly · had | such tran|quillity.

4 For they | suffer · no | pain:
  and their | bodies · are | hale and | fat.

5 They come to no mis|fortune · like | other folk:
  nor | are they | plagued like | other men.

6 Therefore they put on | pride · as a | necklace:
  and clothe themselves in | vio·lence | as · in a | garment.

7 Their eyes shine from | folds of | fatness:
  and they have | all that | heart could | wish.

8 Their talk is | malice · and | mockery:
  and they hand down | slanders | from on | high.

9 Their mouths blas|pheme a·gainst | heaven:
  and their tongues go | to and | fro on | earth.

10 Therefore my | people | turn to them:
  and | find in | them no | fault.

11 They say | 'How can · God | know:
  is there under|standing · in the | Most | High?'

12 Behold | these are · the un|godly:
  yet they | prosper · and in|crease in | riches.

13 Was it for nothing then that I | cleansed my | heart:
  and | washed my | hands in | innocence?

14 Have I been stricken all day | long in | vain:
  and re|buked | every | morning?

† 15 If I had said | 'I will · speak | thus':
  I should have betrayed the | fami·ly | of your | children.

16   Then I thought to under |stand | this:
       but it | was too | hard | for me,

17   Till I went into the | sanctuary · of | God:
       and then I under |stood · what their | end will | be.

18   For you set them in | slipper·y | places:
       and cause them to | fall · from their | treacher·ous | footholds.

19   How suddenly they are | laid | waste:
       they come to an | end they | perish · in | terror.

† 20   As with a dream when | one a |wakes:
       so when you rouse yourself O Lord | you will · de |spise their | image.

21   When my | heart was | soured:
       and I was | wounded | to the | core,

22   I was but | brutish · and | ignorant:
       no | better · than a | beast be |fore you.

23   Nevertheless I am | always | with you:
       for you hold me | by my | right | hand.

24   You will guide me | with your | counsel:
       and afterwards | you will | lead me · to | glory.

25   Whom have I in | heaven · but | you?:
       and there is no one upon earth that I de |sire · in com |parison · with | you.

26   Though my flesh and my | heart | fail me:
       you O | God · are my | portion · for | ever.

27   Behold those who for |sake you · shall | perish:
       and all who whore after other | gods you | will des |troy.

28   But it is good for me to draw | near to | God:
       I have made the Lord God my refuge * and I will tell of | all that | you have | done.

74

JAMES TURLE

1 O Lord our God   why cast us | off so | utterly:
   why does your anger burn a|gainst the | sheep of · your | pasture?

2 Remember your congregation * whom you took to your|self of | old:
   the people that you redeemed to be your own possession *
   and Mount | Zion · where | you have | dwelt.

3 Rouse yourself and go to the | utter | ruins:
   to all the harm that the | enemy · has | done · in the | sanctuary.

4 Your adversaries have made uproar * in the place appointed | for your | praise:
   they have set | up their | standards · in | triumph.

5 They have destroyed on | every | side:
   like those who take axes | up · to a | thicket · of | trees.

6 All the carved woodwork they have | broken | down:
   and | smashed it · with | hammers · and | hatchets.

7 They have set | fire to · your | sanctuary:
   and defiled to the ground the | dwelling·place | of your | name.

8 They have said in their hearts   'Let us make | havoc | of them':
   they have burned down all the holy | places · of | God · in the | land.

9 We see no signs * there is not one | prophet | left:
   there is none who knows how | long these | things shall | be.

10 How long shall the adversary | taunt you · O | God:
   shall the enemy blas|pheme your | name for | ever?

† 11 Why do you hold | back your | hand:
   why do you keep your | right hand | in your | bosom?

12   Yet God is my ˈ king · from of ˈ old:
     who wrought deˈliverance · upˈon the ˈ earth.

13   You divided the ˈ sea · by your ˈ might:
     you shattered the heads of the ˈ dragons ˈ in the ˈ waters.

14   You crushed the ˈ heads · of Leˈviathan:
     and gave him as food to the ˈ creatures · of the ˈ desert ˈ waste.

15   You cleft open ˈ spring and ˈ fountain:
     you dried up the ˈ everˈflowing ˈ waters.

16   The day is yours * and so also ˈ is the ˈ night:
     you have esˈtablished · the ˈ moon · and the ˈ sun.

17   You set all the boundaries ˈ of the ˈ earth:
     you creˈated ˈ winter · and ˈ summer.

18   Remember O Lord the ˈ taunts · of the ˈ enemy:
     how a mindless ˈ people · have blasˈphemed your ˈ name.

19   Do not give to the wild beasts the ˈ soul that ˈ praises you:
     do not forget for ever the ˈ life of ˈ your afˈflicted.

20   Look on all that ˈ you have ˈ made:
     for it is full of darkness * and ˈ violence · inˈhabits · the ˈ earth.

21   Let not the oppressed and reviled turn aˈway reˈjected:
     but let the poor and ˈ needy ˈ praise your ˈ name.

22   Arise O God * plead your ˈ own ˈ cause:
     remember how a mindless people ˈ taunt you ˈ all day ˈ long.

23   Do not forget the ˈ clamour · of your ˈ adversaries:
     or how the shouting of your ˈ enemies · asˈcends conˈtinually.

75

MATTHEW CAMIDGE

1 We give you thanks O God we | give you | thanks:
   we call upon your name * and tell of all the | wonders | you have | done.

2 'I will surely ap|point a | time:
   when I the | Lord will | judge with | equity.

3 'Though the earth shake and | all who | dwell in it:
   it is | I · that have | founded · its | pillars.

4 'I will say to the boasters | "Boast no | more":
   and to the wicked | "Do not | flaunt your | horns;

† 5 ' "Do not flaunt your | horns so | high:
   or speak so | proud and | stiff-|necked." '

6 For there is none from the east or | from the | west:
   or from the wilderness | who can | raise | up;

7 But it is God who | is the | judge:
   who puts down | one · and ex|alts an|other.

8 For there is a cup in the | Lord's | hand:
   and the wine | foams · and is | richly | mixed;

9 He gives it in turn to each of the | wicked · of the | earth:
   they drink it and | drain it | to the | dregs.

10 But I will sing praises to the | God of | Jacob:
   I will | glorify · his | name for | ever.

11 All the horns of the | wicked · I will | break:
   but the horns of the | righteous · shall be | lifted | high.

76

WILLIAM HAVERGAL

1 In Judah ' God is ' known:
   his ' name is ' great in ' Israel:

2 At Salem ' is his ' tabernacle:
   and his ' dwelling ' is in ' Zion.

3 There he broke in pieces the flashing ' arrows · of the ' bow:
   the shield the ' sword · and the ' weapons · of ' battle.

4 Radiant in ' light are ' you:
   greater in majesty ' than · the e'ternal ' hills.

5 The valiant were dumbfounded   they ' sleep their ' sleep:
   and all the men of ' war have ' lost their ' strength.

6 At the blast of your voice O ' God of ' Jacob:
   both horse and ' chariot · were ' cast a'sleep.

7 Terrible are ' you Lord ' God:
   and who may stand be'fore you · when ' you are ' angry?

8 You caused your sentence to be ' heard from ' heaven:
   the earth ' feared ' and was ' still,

9 When God a'rose to ' judgement:
   to ' save · all the ' meek · of the ' earth.

10 For you crushed the ' wrath of ' man:
   you bridled the ' remnant ' of the ' wrathful.

11 O make vows to the Lord your ' God and ' keep them:
   let all around him bring gifts * to him that is ' worthy ' to be ' feared.

12 For he cuts down the ' fury · of ' princes:
   and he is terrible to the ' kings ' of the ' earth.

JONATHAN BATTISHILL

1   I call to my God   I cry ˈ out toˈward him:
    I call to my God   and ˈ surely ˈ he will ˈ answer.

2   In the day of my distress I seek the Lord * I stretch out my hands to ˈ him by ˈ night:
    my soul is poured out without ceasing * it reˈfuses ˈ all ˈ comfort.

3   I think upon God and ˈ groan aˈloud:
    I ˈ muse · and my ˈ spirit ˈ faints.

4   You hold my ˈ eyelids ˈ open:
    I am so ˈ dazed · that I ˈ cannot ˈ flee.

5   I consider the ˈ times · that are ˈ past:
    I remember the ˈ years of ˈ long aˈgo.

6   At night I am ˈ grieved · to the ˈ heart:
    I ponder ˈ and my ˈ spirit · makes ˈ search;

7   'Will the Lord cast us ˈ off for ˈ ever:
    will he ˈ show us · his ˈ favour · no ˈ more?

8   'Is his mercy clean ˈ gone for ˈ ever:
    and his promise come to an ˈ end for ˈ all · generˈations?

9   'Has God forˈgotten · to be ˈ gracious:
    has he shut up his ˈ pity ˈ in disˈpleasure?'

10 And I say * 'Has the right hand of the Most High ˈ lost its ˈ strength:
    has the ˈ arm · of the ˈ Lord ˈ changed?'

11 I will declare the mighty ˈ acts · of the ˈ Lord:
    I will call to ˈ mind your ˈ wonders · of ˈ old.

12 I will think on all that ˈ you have ˈ done:
    and ˈ meditate · upˈon your ˈ works.

13 Your way O ˈ God is ˈ holy:
    who is so ˈ great a ˈ god as ˈ our God?

14 You are the God that ˈ works ˈ wonders:
    you made known your ˈ power aˈmong the ˈ nations;

15 By your mighty arm you reˈdeemed your ˈ people:
    the ˈ children · of ˈ Jacob · and ˈ Joseph.

16 The waters saw you O God * the waters saw you and ˈ were aˈfraid:
    the ˈ depths ˈ also · were ˈ troubled.

17 The clouds poured out water   the ˈ heavens ˈ spoke:
    and your ˈ arrows ˈ darted ˈ forth.

18 The voice of your thunder was ˈ heard · in the ˈ whirlwind:
    your lightnings lit the world * the ˈ earth ˈ shuddered · and ˈ quaked.

19 Your way was in the sea * your path in the ˈ great ˈ waters:
    and your ˈ footsteps ˈ were not ˈ seen.

20 You led your ˈ people · like ˈ sheep:
    by the ˈ hand of ˈ Moses · and ˈ Aaron.

78

J. STAFFORD SMITH

1 Give heed to my teaching | O my | people:
   incline your | ears · to the | words of · my | mouth;

2 For I will open my | mouth · in a | parable:
   and expound the | mysteries · of | former | times.

3 What we have | heard and | known:
   what | our fore|fathers · have | told us,

4 We will not hide from their children * but declare to a generation | yet to | come:
   the praiseworthy acts of the Lord * his | mighty · and | wonder·ful | works.

5 He established a law in Jacob * and made a de|cree in | Israel:
   which he commanded our fore|fathers · to | teach their | children,

6 That future generations might know * and the children | yet un|born:
   that they in turn might | teach it | to their | sons;

7 So that they might put their | confidence · in | God:
   and not forget his | works but | keep · his com|mandments,

8 And not be as their forefathers * a stubborn and re|bellious · gener|ation:
   a generation that did not set their heart aright *
   whose spirit | was not | faithful · to | God.

9 The children of Ephraim | armed · with the | bow:
   turned | back · in the | day of | battle.

10 They did not keep God's covenant * they refused to | walk in · his | law:
   they forgot what he had done * and the | wonders | he had | shown them.

11 For he did marvellous things in the | sight of · their | fathers:
   in the land of Egypt | in the | country · of | Zoan.

12 He divided the sea and | let them · pass | through:
   he made the | waters · stand | up · in a | heap.

13 In the daytime he | led them · with a | cloud:
   and all night | long · with the | light of | fire.

14 He cleft | rocks · in the | wilderness:
   and gave them drink in abundance | as from | springs of | water.

†15 He brought streams | out of · the | rock:
   and caused the waters to | flow | down like | rivers.

J. STAFFORD SMITH

16 But for all this they sinned yet | more a|gainst him:
   and rebelled against the Most | High | in the | desert.

17 They wilfully put | God · to the | test:
   and de|manded | food · for their | appetite.

18 They spoke against | God and | said:
   'Can God prepare a | table | in the | wilderness?

19 'He indeed struck the rock * so that the waters gushed and the | streams · over|flowed:
   but can he also give bread * or provide | meat | for his | people?'

20 When the Lord heard it he was angry * and a fire was kindled a|gainst | Jacob:
   his wrath | blazed a|gainst | Israel.

21 For they put no | trust in | God:
   nor would they be|lieve his | power to | save.

† 22 Then he commanded the | clouds a|bove:
   and | opened · the | doors of | heaven.

23 He rained down manna for | them to | eat:
   and | gave them · the | grain of | heaven.

24 So men ate the | bread of | angels:
   and he | sent them | food · in a|bundance.

80

THOMAS ATTWOOD

1 Hear O Shepherd of Israel * you that led | Joseph · like a | flock:
   you that are enthroned upon the cherubim | shine | out in | glory;

2 Before Ephraim Benjamin | and Man|asseh:
   stir up your | power and | come to | save us.

UNISON † 3 *Restore us again O | Lord of | hosts:*
   show us the light of your countenance | and we | shall be | saved.

4 O Lord | God of | hosts:
   how long will you be | angry · at your | people's | prayer?

5 You have fed them with the | bread of | tears:
   and given them tears to | drink in | good | measure.

6 You have made us the victim | of our | neighbours:
   and our | ene·mies | laugh us · to | scorn.

UNISON 7 *Restore us again O | Lord of | hosts:*
   show us the light of your countenance | and we | shall be | saved.

8 You brought a | vine · out of | Egypt:
   you drove out the | nations · and | planted · it | in.

9 You cleared the | ground be|fore it:
   and it struck | root and | filled the | land.

10 The hills were | cove·red · with its | shadow:
   and its boughs were like the | boughs · of the | great | cedars.

11 It stretched out its | branches · to the | sea:
   and its tender | shoots · to the | Great | River.

12 Why then have you broken | down its | walls:
   so that every passer-|by can | pluck its | fruit?

13 The wild boar out of the woods | roots it | up:
   and the locusts from the | wild | places · de|vour it.

14 Turn to us again O | Lord of | hosts:
   look | down from | heaven · and | see.

15 Bestow your care up|on this | vine:
   the stock which your | own right | hand has | planted.

16 As for those that burn it with fire and | cut it | down:
    let them perish at the re|buke | of your | countenance.

17 Let your power rest on the man at your | right | hand:
    on that son of man whom you | made so | strong · for your|self.

18 And so we shall | not turn | back from you:
    give us life   and we will | call up|on your | name.

UNISON 19 *Restore us again O | Lord of | hosts:*
    show us the light of your countenance | and we | shall be | saved.

81

EDWARD J. HOPKINS

1 O sing joyfully to ' God our ' strength:
   shout in ' triumph · to the ' God of ' Jacob.

2 Make music and ' beat up·on the ' drum:
   sound the ' lute and · the mel'odi·ous ' harp.

3 Blow the ram's horn at the ' new ' moon:
   and at the full moon ' of our ' day of ' festival.

4 For this was a ' statute · for ' Israel:
   a com'mandment · of the ' God of ' Jacob,

† 5 Which he laid on Joseph as a ' solemn ' charge:
   when he came ' out of · the ' land of ' Egypt.

6 I heard a voice that I had not ' known ' saying:
   'I eased your shoulders of the burden *
      and your ' hands were ' freed · from the ' load.

7 'You called to me in trouble ' and I ' rescued you:
   I answered you from the secret place of my thunder *
      I put you to the ' test · at the ' waters · of ' Meribah.

8 'Listen my people and ' I · will ad'monish you:
   O Israel if ' only ' you would ' hear me.

9 'There shall be no strange ' god a'mong you:
   nor shall you bow ' down · to an ' ali·en ' god.

† 10 'I am the Lord your God * who brought you up from the ' land of ' Egypt:
   open wide your ' mouth and ' I will ' fill it.

11 'But my people would not ' listen · to my ' voice:
   and ' Israel ' would have ' none of me.

12 'So I left them to the stubbornness ' of their ' hearts:
   to walk ac'cording · to their ' own de'signs.

13 'If only my ' people · would ' listen:
   if Israel ' would but ' walk in · my ' ways,

14 'I would soon put ' down their ' enemies:
   and turn my ' hand a'gainst their ' adversaries.

15 'Those that hate the Lord would | cringe be|fore him:
and their | punishment · would | last for | ever.

16 'But Israel I would feed with the | finest | wheat:
and satisfy you with | honey | from the | rocks.'

82

J. HARRISON

1 God has stood up in the | council · of | heaven:
in the midst of the | gods | he gives | judgement.

2 'How long will you | judge un|justly:
and | favour · the | cause · of the | wicked?

3 'Judge for the | poor and | fatherless:
vindicate the af|flicted | and op|pressed.

4 'Rescue the | poor and | needy:
and | save them · from the | hands · of the | wicked.

5 'They do not know   they do not understand *
they walk a|bout in | darkness:
all the found|ations · of the | earth are | shaken.

6 'Therefore I say | "Though · you are | gods:
and all of you | sons · of the | Most | High,

7 ' "Nevertheless you shall | die like | man:
and | fall like | one of · the | princes." '

157

J. HARRISON

8 Arise O God and | judge the | earth:
for you shall take all | nations · as | your pos|session.

84

Edward C. Bairstow

1 How lovely ǀ is your ǀ dwelling-place:
   O ǀ Lord ǀ God of ǀ hosts!

2 My soul has a desire and longing to enter the ǀ courts · of the ǀ Lord:
   my heart and my flesh reǀjoice · in the ǀ living ǀ God.

3 The sparrow has found her a home *
      and the swallow a nest where she may ǀ lay her ǀ young:
   even your altar   O Lord of ǀ hosts my ǀ King · and my ǀ God.

4 Blessèd are those who ǀ dwell in · your ǀ house:
   they will ǀ always · be ǀ praising ǀ you.

5 Blessèd is the man whose ǀ strength · is in ǀ you:
   in whose ǀ heart · are the ǀ highways · to ǀ Zion;

6 Who going through the valley of dryness * finds there a spring from ǀ which to ǀ drink:
   till the autumn ǀ rain shall ǀ clothe it · with ǀ blessings.

† 7 They go from ǀ strength to ǀ strength:
   they appear every one of them before the ǀ God of ǀ gods in ǀ Zion.

8 O Lord God of hosts ǀ hear my ǀ prayer:
   give ǀ ear O ǀ God of ǀ Jacob.

9 Behold O God ǀ him who · reigns ǀ over us:
   and look upon the ǀ face of ǀ your aǀnointed.

10 One day in your courts is ǀ better · than a ǀ thousand:
   I would rather stand at the threshold of the house of my God *
      than ǀ dwell · in the ǀ tents of · unǀgodliness.

11 For the Lord God is a rampart and a shield * the Lord gives ǀ favour · and ǀ honour:
   and no good thing will he withhold from ǀ those who ǀ walk in ǀ innocence.

† 12 O Lord ǀ God of ǀ hosts:
   blessèd is the man who ǀ puts his ǀ trust in ǀ you.

85

THOMAS HANFORTH

1 O Lord you were gracious ˈ to your ˈ land:
   you reˈstored the ˈ fortunes · of ˈ Jacob.

2 You forgave the iniquity ˈ of your ˈ people:
   and ˈ covered ˈ all their ˈ sin.

3 You put aside ˈ all your ˈ wrath:
   and turned away from your ˈ fierce ˈ indigˈnation.

4 Return to us again O ˈ God our ˈ saviour:
   and ˈ let your ˈ anger ˈ cease from us.

5 Will you be displeased with ˈ us for ˈ ever;
   will you stretch out your wrath * from one geneˈration ˈ to anˈother?

6 Will you not give us ˈ life aˈgain:
   that your ˈ people ˈ may reˈjoice in you?

† 7 Show us your ˈ mercy · O ˈ Lord:
   and ˈ grant us ˈ your salˈvation.

8 I will hear what the Lord ˈ God will ˈ speak:
   for he will speak peace to his people *
      to his faithful ones whose ˈ hearts are ˈ turned to ˈ him.

9 Truly his salvation is near to ˈ those that ˈ fear him:
   and his ˈ glory · shall ˈ dwell · in our ˈ land.

10 Mercy and truth are ˈ met toˈgether:
   righteousness and ˈ peace have ˈ kissed each ˈ other;

11 Truth shall flourish ˈ out of · the ˈ earth:
   and righteousness ˈ shall look ˈ down from ˈ heaven.

12 The Lord will also give us ˈ all · that is ˈ good:
   and our ˈ land shall ˈ yield its ˈ plenty.

13 For righteousness shall ˈ go beˈfore him:
   and tread the ˈ path beˈfore his ˈ feet.

86

JOHN FOSTER

1   Incline your ear to me O ' God and ' answer me:
      for ' I am ' poor · and in ' misery.

2   Preserve my life for ' I am ' faithful:
      my God save your servant who ' puts his ' trust in ' you.

3   Be merciful to ' me O ' Lord:
      for I ' call to · you ' all the · day ' long.

4   O make glad the ' soul of · your ' servant:
      for I put my ' hope in ' you O ' Lord.

5   For you Lord are ' good · and for'giving:
      of great and continuing kindness to ' all who ' call up'on you.

6   Hear my ' prayer O ' Lord:
      and give heed to the ' voice · of my ' suppli'cation.

† 7   In the day of my trouble I ' call up'on you:
      for ' you will ' surely ' answer.

8   Among the gods there is none like ' you O ' Lord:
      nor are there ' any ' deeds like ' yours.

9   All the nations you have made shall come and ' worship · be'fore you:
      O Lord they shall ' glori'fy your ' name.

10   For you are great and do ' marvel·lous ' things:
      and ' you a'lone are ' God.

11   Show me your way O Lord   and I will ' walk in · your ' truth:
      let my heart de'light to ' fear your ' name.

12   I will praise you O Lord my God with ' all my ' heart:
      and I will ' glorify · your ' name for ' ever.

13   For great is your abiding ' love to'ward me:
      and you have delivered my life from the ' lowest ' depths · of the ' grave.

14   Insolent men O God have ' risen · a'gainst me:
      a band of ruthless men seek my life * they have not set ' God be'fore their ' eyes.

15   But you Lord are a God ' gracious · and com'passionate:
      slow to anger ' full of ' goodness · and ' truth.

16 Turn to me and be merciful * give your | strength · to your | servant:
 and | save the | son of · your | handmaid.

17 Show me some token | of your | goodness:
 that those who hate me may see it and be ashamed *
 because you Lord are my | helper | and my | comforter.

87

161

1 He has founded it upon a | holy | hill:
 and the Lord loves the gates of Zion more than | all the | dwellings · of | Jacob.

2 Glorious things shall be | spoken · of | you:
 O Zion | city | of our | God.

3 I might speak of my kinsmen in Egypt | or in | Babylon:
 in Philistia Tyre or Nubia | where | each was | born.

4 But of Zion it | shall be | said:
 many were born in her * he that is Most | High | has es|tablished her.

5 When the Lord draws up the record | of the | nations:
 he shall take note where | every | man was | born.

6 And the singers and the | dancers · to|gether:
 shall | make their | song · to your | name.

88

LUKE FLINTOFT

1   O Lord my God   I call for ˈ help by ˈ day:
     and by night also I ˈ cry ˈ out beˈfore you.

2   Let my prayer come ˈ into · your ˈ presence:
     and turn your ˈ ear · to my ˈ loud ˈ crying.

† 3   For my soul is ˈ filled with ˈ trouble:
     and my life has come ˈ even · to the ˈ brink · of the ˈ grave.

4   I am reckoned among those that go ˈ down · to the ˈ Pit:
     I am a ˈ man that ˈ has no ˈ help.

5   I lie among the dead * like the slain that ˈ sleep · in the ˈ grave:
     whom you remember no more * who are cut ˈ off ˈ from your ˈ power.

6   You have laid me in the ˈ lowest ˈ Pit:
     in darkness and ˈ in the ˈ water·y ˈ depths.

7   Your wrath lies ˈ heavy · upˈon me:
     and all your ˈ waves are ˈ brought aˈgainst me.

8   You have put my ˈ friends far ˈ from me:
     and made me to ˈ be abˈhorred ˈ by them.

9   I am so fast in prison I ˈ cannot · get ˈ free:
     my eyes fail beˈcause of ˈ my afˈfliction.

10   Lord I call to you ˈ every ˈ day:
     I stretch ˈ out my ˈ hands toˈward you.

11   Will you work ˈ wonders · for the ˈ dead:
     or will the shades rise ˈ up aˈgain to ˈ praise you?

12   Shall your love be deˈclared · in the ˈ grave:
     or your faithfulness ˈ in the ˈ place · of deˈstruction?

13   Will your wonders be made ˈ known · in the ˈ dark:
     or your righteousness in the land where ˈ all things ˈ are forˈgotten?

14   But to you Lord ˈ will I ˈ cry:
     early in the morning my ˈ prayer shall ˈ come beˈfore you.

15   O Lord why have ˈ you reˈjected me:
     why do you ˈ hide your ˈ face ˈ from me?

16 I have been afflicted and wearied from my | youth | upward:
    I am tossed high and | low   I | cease to | be.

17 Your fierce anger has | over|whelmed me:
    and your | terrors · have | put me · to | silence.

18 They surround me like a flood | all the · day | long:
    they close up|on me · from | every | side.

19 Friend and acquaintance you have put | far | from me:
    and kept my com|panions | from my | sight.

89

163
EDWARD J. HOPKINS

1 Lord I will sing for ever of your | loving-|kindnesses:
   my mouth shall proclaim your faithfulness through|out all | gener|ations.

2 I have said of your loving-kindness that it is | built for | ever:
   you have established your | faithful·ness | in the | heavens.

3 The Lord said   'I have made a covenant | with my | chosen:
   I have sworn an | oath · to my | servant | David.

4 'I will establish your | line for | ever:
   and build up your | throne for | all · gener|ations.'

5 Let the heavens praise your | wonders · O | Lord:
   and let your faithfulness be sung in the as|sembly | of the | holy ones.

6 For who amidst the clouds can be com|pared · to the | Lord:
   or who is like the Lord a|mong the | sons of | heaven?

7 A God to be feared in the council | of the | holy ones:
   great and terrible above | all that | are a|round him.

8 O Lord God of hosts | who is | like you?:
   your power and your | faithfulness · are | all a|bout you.

9 You rule the | raging · of the | sea:
   when its | waves | surge you | still them.

10 You crushed Rahab | like a | carcase:
   you scattered your enemies | by your | mighty | arm.

continued

129

EDWARD J. HOPKINS

11 The heavens are yours * so also | is the | earth:
   you founded the | world and | all · that is | in it.

12 You created the | north · and the | south:
   Tabor and Mount | Hermon · shall | sing of · your | name.

13 Mighty | is your | arm:
   strong is your hand * and your right | hand is | lifted | high.

14 Righteousness and justice are the foundation | of your | throne:
   loving-kindness and | faithfulness · at|tend your | presence.

15 Happy the people who know the tri|umphal | shout:
   who walk O | Lord · in the | light of · your | countenance.

16 They rejoice all the day long be|cause of · your | name:
   because of your | righteousness · they | are ex|alted.

17 For you are their glory | and their | strength:
   and our heads are up|lifted | by your | favour.

18 Our king be|longs · to the | Lord:
   he that rules over us to the | Holy | One of | Israel.

19 You spoke | once · in a | vision:
   and | said | to your | faithful one,

20 'I have set a youth a|bove a | warrior:
   I have exalted a | young man | out of · the | people.

21 'I have found my | servant | David:
   and anointed him | with my | holy | oil.

22 'My hand | shall up|hold him:
   and my | arm | shall | strengthen him.

23 'No enemy | shall de|ceive him:
   no | evil | man shall | hurt him.

24 'I will crush his | adversaries · be|fore him:
   and | strike down | those that | hate him.

25 'My faithfulness and loving-kindness | shall be | with him:
   and through my name his | head · shall be | lifted | high.

26 'I will set the hand of his dominion upon the | Western | Sea:
   and his right hand shall stretch to the | streams of | Meso·po|tamia.

EDWARD J. HOPKINS

27 'He will call to me | "You · are my | Father:
   my God and the | Rock of | my sal|vation.''

28 'I will make him my | first-born | son:
   and highest a|mong the | kings · of the | earth.

29 'I will ever maintain my loving-|kindness · to|ward him:
   and my covenant | with him · shall | stand | firm.

30 'I will establish his | line for | ever:
   and his | throne · like the | days of | heaven.

31 'If his children for|sake my | law:
   and | will not | walk in · my | judgements;

32 'If they pro|fane my | statutes:
   and | do not | keep · my com|mandments,

33 'Then I will punish their re|bellion · with the | rod:
   and | their in|iquity · with | blows.

34 'But I will not cause my loving-|kindness · to | cease from him:
   nor will | I be|tray my | faithfulness.

35 'I will not pro|fane my | covenant:
   or alter | what has | passed from · my | lips.

36 'Once and for all I have | sworn · by my | holiness:
   I will | not prove | false to | David.

37 'His posterity shall en|dure for | ever:
   and his throne be | as the | sun be|fore me;

38 'Like the moon that is es|tablished · for | ever:
   and stands in the | heavens · for | ever|more.'

90

FREDERICK A. J. HERVEY

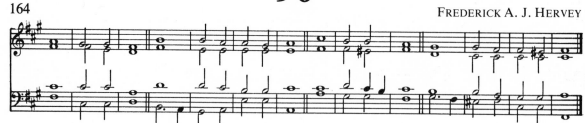

1 Lord you have | been our | refuge:
   from one gener|ation | to an|other.

2 Before the mountains were born * or the earth and the world were | brought to | be:
   from eternity to e|terni·ty | you are | God.

3 You turn man | back · into | dust:
   saying   'Return to | dust you | sons of | Adam.'

4 For a thousand years in your sight are like | yester·day | passing:
   or | like one | watch · of the | night.

5 You cut them | short · like a | dream:
   like the fresh | grass | of the | morning;

6 In the morning it is | green and | flourishes:
   at evening it is | withered · and | dried | up.

7 And we are con|sumed · by your | anger:
   because of your indig|nation · we | cease to | be.

8 You have brought our in|iquities · be|fore you:
   and our secret | sins · to the | light of · your | countenance.

9 Our days decline be|neath your | wrath:
   and our years | pass a|way · like a | sigh.

10 The days of our life are three score years and ten * or if we have | strength four | score:
   the pride of our labours is but toil and sorrow *
     for it passes quickly a|way and | we are | gone.

11 Who can know the | power of · your | wrath:
   who can know your indig|nation · like | those that | fear you?

12 Teach us so to | number · our | days:
   that we may ap|ply our | hearts to | wisdom.

THOMAS KELWAY

13 Relent O Lord * how long will | you be | angry?:
    take | pity | on your | servants.

14 O satisfy us early | with your | mercy:
    that all our days we | may re|joice and | sing.

15 Give us joy for all the days you | have af|flicted us:
    for the | years · we have | suffered · ad|versity.

16 Show your | servants · your | work:
    and let their | children | see your | glory.

17 May the gracious favour of the Lord our | God · be up|on us:
    prosper the work of our hands * O | prosper · the | work · of our | hands!

91

RICHARD WOODWARD

1 He who dwells in the shelter of the | Most | High:
   who abides under the | shadow | of the · Al|mighty,

2 He will say to the Lord * 'You are my refuge | and my | stronghold:
   my | God in | whom I | trust.'

3 For he will deliver you from the | snare · of the | hunter:
   and | from the · de|stroying | curse.

4 He will cover you with his wings * and you will be safe | under · his | feathers:
   his faithfulness will | be your | shield · and de|fence.

5 You shall not be afraid of any | terror · by | night:
   or of the | arrow · that | flies by | day,

6 Of the pestilence that walks a|bout in | darkness:
   or the | plague · that de|stroys at | noonday.

7 A thousand may fall beside you * and ten thousand at your | right | hand:
   but | you it | shall not | touch;

8 Your own | eyes shall | see:
   and look on the re|ward | of the · un|godly.

9 The Lord him|self · is your | refuge:
   you have | made the · Most | High your | stronghold.

10 Therefore no | harm · will be|fall you:
   nor will any | scourge come | near your | tent.

11 For he will com|mand his | angels:
   to | keep you · in | all your | ways.

12 They will bear you | up · in their | hands:
   lest you dash your | foot a|gainst a | stone.

13 You will tread on the | lion · and the | adder:
   the young lion and the serpent you will | trample | under | foot.

14 'He has set his love upon me * and therefore I | will de|liver him:
   I will lift him out of danger be|cause · he has | known my | name.

15 'When he calls upon me | I will | answer him:
   I will be with him in trouble * I will | rescue him · and | bring him · to | honour.

16 'With long | life · I will | satisfy him:
   and | fill him · with | my sal|vation.'

92

PERCY C. BUCK

1 How good to give | thanks · to the | Lord:
   to sing praises to your | name | O Most | High,

2 To declare your | love · in the | morning:
   and at | night to | sing of · your | faithfulness,

† 3 Upon the lute   upon the lute of | ten | strings:
   and to the | melo·dy | of the | lyre.

4 For in all you have done O Lord you have | made me | glad:
   I will sing for joy be|cause of · the | works · of your | hands.

5 Lord how glorious | are your | works:
   your | thoughts are | very | deep.

6 The brutish do | not con|sider:
   and the | fool · cannot | under|stand

7 That though the wicked | sprout like | grass:
   and | all wrong|doers | flourish,

8 They flourish to be de|stroyed · for | ever:
   but you Lord are ex|alted · for | ever|more.

9 For behold   your enemies O Lord your | enemies · shall | perish:
   and all the workers of | wicked·ness | shall be | scattered.

10 You have lifted up my head * like the horns of the | wild | oxen:
   I am an|ointed · with | fresh | oil;

11 My eyes have looked | down · on my | enemies:
   and my ears have heard the ruin of | those who · rose | up a|gainst me.

12 The righteous shall | flourish · like the | palm tree:
   they shall spread a|broad · like a | cedar · in | Lebanon;

13 For they are planted in the | house · of the | Lord:
   and flourish in the | courts of | our | God.

14 In old age they shall be | full of | sap:
   they shall be | sturdy · and | laden · with | branches;

15 And they will say that the | Lord is | just:
   the Lord my Rock in | whom is | no un|righteousness.

93

168

EDWIN G. MONK

1 The Lord is King * and has put on ˈ robes of ˈ glory:
   the Lord has put on his glory * he has ˈ girded · himˈself with ˈ strength.

2 He has made the ˈ world so ˈ firm:
   that it ˈ cannot ˈ be ˈ moved.

3 Your throne is esˈtablished · from of ˈ old:
   you ˈ are from ˈ everˈlasting.

4 The floods have lifted up O Lord * the floods have lifted ˈ up their ˈ voice:
   the ˈ floods lift ˈ up their ˈ pounding.

5 But mightier than the sound of many waters *
      than the mighty waters or the ˈ breakers · of the ˈ sea:
   the ˈ Lord on ˈ high is ˈ mighty.

6 Your decrees are ˈ very ˈ sure:
   and holiness O Lord aˈdorns your ˈ house for ˈ ever.

94

169

SAMUEL WESLEY

1 O Lord God to whom ˈ vengeance · beˈlongs:
   O God to whom vengeance beˈlongs shine ˈ out in ˈ glory.

2 Arise ˈ judge · of the ˈ earth:
   and requite the ˈ proud as ˈ they deˈserve.

3 Lord how ˈ long · shall the ˈ wicked:
   how ˈ long · shall the ˈ wicked ˈ triumph?

4 How long shall all evildoers ˈ pour out ˈ words:
   how ˈ long · shall they ˈ boast and ˈ flaunt themselves?

5 They crush your ˈ people · O ˈ Lord:
    they opˈpress your ˈ own posˈsession.

6 They murder the ˈ widow · and the ˈ alien:
    they ˈ put the ˈ fatherless · to ˈ death.

7 And they say 'The ˈ Lord · does not ˈ see:
    nor does the ˈ God of ˈ Jacob · conˈsider it.'

8 Consider this   you senseless aˈmong the ˈ people:
    fools ˈ when · will you ˈ underˈstand?

9 He who planted the ear   does ˈ he not ˈ hear:
    he who formed the ˈ eye   does ˈ he not ˈ see?

10 He who disciplines the nations will ˈ he not ˈ punish:
    has the ˈ teacher · of manˈkind no ˈ knowledge?

† 11 The Lord knows the ˈ thoughts of ˈ man:
    he ˈ knows · that they ˈ are mere ˈ breath.

12 Blessèd is the man whom you ˈ discipline · O ˈ Lord:
    and ˈ teach ˈ from your ˈ law,

13 Giving him rest from ˈ days of ˈ misery:
    till a ˈ pit is ˈ dug · for the ˈ wicked.

14 The Lord will not cast ˈ off his ˈ people:
    nor ˈ will he · forˈsake his ˈ own.

15 For justice shall return to the ˈ righteous ˈ man:
    and with him to ˈ all the ˈ true of ˈ heart.

16 Who will stand up for me aˈgainst the ˈ wicked:
    who will take my part aˈgainst the ˈ evilˈdoers?

17 If the Lord had not ˈ been my ˈ helper:
    I would soon have ˈ dwelt · in the ˈ land of ˈ silence.

18 But when I said 'My ˈ foot has ˈ slipped':
    your ˈ mercy · O ˈ Lord was ˈ holding me.

19 In all the ˈ doubts · of my ˈ heart:
    your consolˈations · deˈlighted · my ˈ soul.

20 Will you be any friend to the ˈ court of ˈ wickedness:
    that contrives ˈ evil · by ˈ means of ˈ law?   *continued*

21 They band together against the ˈ life · of the ˈ righteous:
    and conˈdemn ˈ inno·cent ˈ blood.

22 But the ˈ Lord · is my ˈ stronghold:
    my ˈ God · is my ˈ rock · and my ˈ refuge.

23 Let him requite them for their wickedness * and silence them ˈ for their ˈ evil:
    the ˈ Lord our ˈ God shall ˈ silence them.

95

170   RICHARD GOODSON

1 O come let us sing ˈ out · to the ˈ Lord:
   let us shout in triumph to the ˈ rock of ˈ our salˈvation.

2 Let us come before his ˈ face with ˈ thanksgiving:
   and cry ˈ out to · him ˈ joyfully · in ˈ psalms.

3 For the Lord is a ˈ great ˈ God:
   and a great ˈ king a·bove ˈ all ˈ gods.

4 In his hand are the ˈ depths · of the ˈ earth:
   and the peaks of the ˈ mountains · are ˈ his ˈ also.

5 The sea is his and ˈ he ˈ made it:
   his hands ˈ moulded ˈ dry ˈ land.

6 Come let us worship and ˈ bow ˈ down:
   and kneel beˈfore the ˈ Lord our ˈ maker.

7 For he is the ˈ Lord our ˈ God:
   we are his ˈ people · and the ˈ sheep of · his ˈ pasture.

96

ROBERT COOKE

1 O sing to the Lord a | new | song:
   sing to the | Lord | all the | earth.

2 Sing to the Lord and bless his | holy | name:
   proclaim the good news of his sal|vation · from | day to | day.

3 Declare his glory a|mong the | nations:
   and his | wonders · a|mong all | peoples.

4 For great is the Lord and | greatly · to be | praised:
   he is more to be | feared than | all | gods.

5 As for all the gods of the nations | they are · mere | idols:
   it is the | Lord who | made the | heavens.

6 Majesty and | glory · are be|fore him:
   beauty and | power are | in his | sanctuary.

7 Render to the Lord you families | of the | nations:
   render to the | Lord | glory · and | might.

8 Render to the Lord the honour | due · to his | name:
   bring offerings and | come in|to his | courts.

9 O worship the Lord in the beauty | of his | holiness:
   let the whole earth | stand in | awe of | him.

10 Say among the nations that the | Lord is | king:
   he has made the world so firm that it can never be moved *
      and he shall | judge the | peoples · with | equity.

11 Let the heavens rejoice   and let the | earth be | glad:
   let the sea | roar and | all that | fills it;

12 Let the fields rejoice and | every·thing | in them:
   then shall all the trees of the wood shout with | joy be|fore the | Lord;

† 13 For he comes   he comes to | judge the | earth:
   he shall judge the world with righteousness * and the | peoples | with his | truth.

97

HENRY T. SMART

1 The Lord is king   let the | earth re|joice.
   let the | multitude · of | islands · be | glad.

2 Clouds and darkness are | round a|bout him:
   righteousness and justice are the found|ation | of his | throne.

3 Fire | goes be|fore him:
   and burns up his | enemies · on | every | side.

4 His lightnings | light the | world:
   the | earth | sees it · and | quakes.

5 The mountains melt like wax be|fore his | face:
   from before the face of the | Lord of | all the | earth.

6 The heavens have pro|claimed his | righteousness:
   and all | peoples · have | seen his | glory.

7 They are ashamed * all those who serve idols and glory in | mere | nothings:
   all | gods bow | down be|fore him.

8 Zion heard and was glad * and the daughters of | Judah · re|joiced:
   be|cause of · your | judgements · O | God.

9 For you Lord are most high over | all the | earth:
   you are exalted | far a·bove | all | gods.

10 The Lord loves | those that · hate | evil:
    the Lord guards the life of the faithful *
    and delivers them from the | hand of | the un|godly.

11 Light | dawns · for the | righteous:
    and | joy · for the | true of | heart.

12 Rejoice in the | Lord you | righteous:
    and give | thanks · to his | holy | name.

98

GEORGE J. ELVEY

1 O sing to the Lord a | new | song:
   for he has | done | marvel·lous | things;

2 His right hand and his | holy | arm:
   they have | got | him the | victory.

3 The Lord has made | known · his sal|vation:
   he has revealed his just de|liverance · in the | sight of · the | nations.

4 He has remembered his mercy and faithfulness towards the | house of | Israel:
   and all the ends of the earth have seen the sal|vation | of our | God.

5 Shout with joy to the Lord | all the | earth:
   break into | singing · and | make | melody.

6 Make melody to the Lord up|on the | harp:
   upon the harp and | with the | sounds of | praise.

7 With trumpets | and with | horns:
   cry out in triumph be|fore the | Lord the | king.

8 Let the sea roar and | all that | fills it:
   the good earth and | those who | live up|on it.

9 Let the rivers | clap their | hands:
   and let the mountains ring out to|gether · be|fore the | Lord;

10 For he comes to | judge the | earth:
   he shall judge the world with righteousness * and the | peoples | with | equity.

99

174   JONATHAN BATTISHILL

1 The Lord is king   let the | nations | tremble:
   he is enthroned upon the cherubim | let the | earth | quake.

2 The Lord is | great in | Zion:
   he is | high a|bove all | nations.

3 Let them praise your great and | terri·ble | name:
   for | holy | is the | Lord.

4 The Mighty One is king and | loves | justice:
   you have established equity *
    you have dealt | righteousness · and | justice · in | Jacob.

UNISON   5 *O exalt the | Lord our | God:*
   and bow down before his |footstool · for | he is | holy.

6 Moses and Aaron among his priests *
   and Samuel among those who call up|on his | name:
   they called to the | Lord | and he | answered.

7 He spoke to them from the | pillar · of | cloud:
   they kept to his teachings | and the | law · that he | gave them.

8 You answered them O | Lord our | God:
   you were a forgiving God to them *
   and | pardoned · their | wrong|doing.

UNISON   9 *O exalt the | Lord our | God:*
   *and bow down towards his holy hill ***
    for the | Lord our | God is | holy.

100

175

GEORGE A. MACFARREN

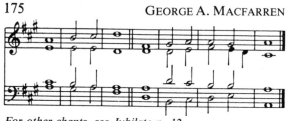

For other chants, see Jubilate p. 12

1 O shout to the Lord in triumph ǀ all the ǀ earth:
serve the Lord with gladness * and come before his ǀ face with ǀ songs of ǀ joy.

2 Know that the Lord ǀ he is ǀ God:
it is he who has made us and we are his *
we are his ǀ people · and the ǀ sheep of · his ǀ pasture.

3 Come into his gates with thanksgiving * and into his ǀ courts with ǀ praise:
give thanks to him and ǀ bless his ǀ holy ǀ name.

4 For the Lord is good * his loving mercy ǀ is for ǀ ever:
his faithfulness through ǀ out all ǀ gener ǀ ations.

101

176

THOMAS ATTWOOD

1 My song shall be of ǀ steadfastness · and ǀ justice:
to ǀ you Lord ǀ will I ǀ sing.

2 I will be wise in the ǀ way of ǀ innocence:
O ǀ when ǀ will you ǀ come to me?

3 I will walk with ǀ in my ǀ house:
in ǀ puri ǀ ty of ǀ heart.

4 I will set nothing evil be ǀ fore my ǀ eyes:
I hate the sin of backsliders   it shall ǀ get no ǀ hold ǀ on me.

† 5 Crookedness of heart shall de ǀ part ǀ from me:
I will ǀ know ǀ nothing · of ǀ wickedness.

[6 The man who secretly slanders his neighbour I ǀ will de ǀ stroy:
the proud look and the arrogant ǀ heart · I will ǀ not en ǀ dure.]

continued

THOMAS ATTWOOD

7 My eyes shall look to the faithful in the land *
 and they shall ˈ make their ˈ home with me:
 one who walks in the way of innocence ˈ he shall ˈ minisˑter ˈ to me.

8 No man who practises deceit shall ˈ live in · my ˈ house:
 no one who utters ˈ lies shall ˈ stand in · my ˈ sight.

[9 Morning by morning I will destroy all the ˈ wicked · of the ˈ land:
 and cut off all evildoers from the ˈ city ˈ of the ˈ Lord.]

102

177

JOHN GOSS

1 O Lord ˈ hear my ˈ prayer:
 and ˈ let my ˈ cry ˈ come to you.

2 Do not hide your face from me in the ˈ day of · my ˈ trouble:
 turn your ear to me * and when I ˈ call be ˈ swift to ˈ answer.

3 For my days pass aˈway like ˈ smoke:
 and my bones ˈ burn as ˈ in a ˈ furnace.

4 My heart is scorched and ˈ withered · like ˈ grass:
 and I forˈget to ˈ eat my ˈ bread.

5 I am weary with the ˈ sound of · my ˈ groaning:
 my ˈ bones stick ˈ fast to · my ˈ skin.

6 I have become like an ˈ owl · in the ˈ wilderness:
 like a ˈ screech-owl · aˈmong the ˈ ruins.

7 I keep watch   and ˈ flit · to and ˈ fro:
 like a ˈ sparrow · upˈon a ˈ housetop.

8 My enemies taunt me ˈ all day ˈ long:
 and those who ˈ rave at me · make ˈ oaths aˈgainst me.

9 Surely I have eaten ˈ ashes · for ˈ bread:
 and ˈ mingled · my ˈ drink with ˈ tears,

10　Because of your wrath and ˈ indigˈnation:
　　for you have taken me ˈ up and ˈ tossed · me aˈside.

† 11　My days deˈcline · like a ˈ shadow:
　　and I ˈ wither · aˈway like ˈ grass.

12　But you Lord are enˈthroned for ˈ ever:
　　and your name shall be known throughˈout all ˈ generˈations.

13　You will arise and have ˈ mercy up·on ˈ Zion:
　　for it is time to pity her　the apˈpointed ˈ time has ˈ come.

14　Your servants love ˈ even · her ˈ stones:
　　and her ˈ dust moves ˈ them to ˈ pity.

15　Then shall the nations fear your ˈ name O ˈ Lord:
　　and all the ˈ kings · of the ˈ earth your ˈ glory,

16　When the Lord has ˈ built up ˈ Zion:
　　when he ˈ shows himˈself · in his ˈ glory,

17　When he turns to the ˈ prayer · of the ˈ destitute:
　　and does not deˈspise their ˈ suppliˈcation.

† 18　Let this be written down for ˈ those who · come ˈ after:
　　and a people yet unˈborn will ˈ praise the ˈ Lord.

19　For the Lord has looked down from the ˈ height · of his ˈ holiness:
　　from heaven he has ˈ looked upˈon the ˈ earth,

20　To hear the ˈ groaning · of the ˈ prisoner:
　　to deliver ˈ those conˈdemned to ˈ die;

21　That they may proclaim the name of the ˈ Lord in ˈ Zion:
　　and his ˈ praises ˈ in Jeˈrusalem,

22　When the nations are ˈ gathered · toˈgether:
　　and the ˈ kingdoms · to ˈ serve the ˈ Lord.

23　He has broken my strength beˈfore my ˈ time:
　　he has ˈ cut ˈ short my ˈ days.

24　Do not take me away O God in the ˈ midst of · my ˈ life:
　　you whose years exˈtend through ˈ all · generˈations.

25　In the beginning you laid the founˈdations · of the ˈ earth:
　　and the ˈ heavens · are the ˈ work of · your ˈ hands.

26　They shall perish　but ˈ you · will enˈdure:
　　they shall all grow old like a garment *
　　　like clothes you will change them and ˈ they shall ˈ pass aˈway.

27　But you are the ˈ same for ˈ ever:
　　and your ˈ years will ˈ never ˈ fail.

28　The children of your servants shall ˈ rest seˈcure:
　　and their seed shall be esˈtablished ˈ in your ˈ sight.

103

SAMUEL WESLEY

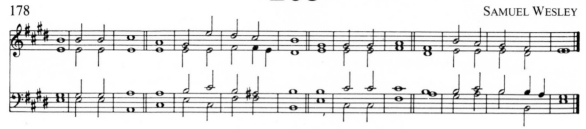

1   Praise the Lord ᐧ O my ᐧ soul:
    and all that is within me ᐧ praise his ᐧ holy ᐧ name.

2   Praise the Lord ᐧ O my ᐧ soul:
    and for'get not ᐧ all his ᐧ benefits,

3   Who forgives ᐧ all your ᐧ sin:
    and ᐧ heals ᐧ all · your in'firmities,

4   Who redeems your ᐧ life · from the ᐧ Pit:
    and crowns you with ᐧ mercy ᐧ and com'passion;

† 5   Who satisfies your being with ᐧ good ᐧ things:
    so that your ᐧ youth · is re'newed · like an ᐧ eagle's.

6   The Lord ᐧ works ᐧ righteousness:
    and justice for ᐧ all who ᐧ are op'pressed.

7   He made known his ᐧ ways to ᐧ Moses:
    and his ᐧ works · to the ᐧ children · of ᐧ Israel.

8   The Lord is full of com'passion · and ᐧ mercy:
    slow to anger ᐧ and of ᐧ great ᐧ goodness.

9   He will not ᐧ always · be ᐧ chiding:
    nor will he ᐧ keep his ᐧ anger · for ᐧ ever.

10   He has not dealt with us ac'cording · to our ᐧ sins:
    nor rewarded us ac'cording ᐧ to our ᐧ wickedness.

11   For as the heavens are high a'bove the ᐧ earth:
    so great is his ᐧ mercy · over ᐧ those that ᐧ fear him;

12   As far as the east is ᐧ from the ᐧ west:
    so far has he ᐧ set our ᐧ sins ᐧ from us.

13   As a father is tender to'wards his ᐧ children:
    so is the Lord ᐧ tender · to ᐧ those that ᐧ fear him.

† 14   For he knows of ᐧ what · we are ᐧ made:
    he re'members · that we ᐧ are but ᐧ dust.

15   The days of man are ᐧ but as ᐧ grass:
    he flourishes ᐧ like a ᐧ flower · of the ᐧ field;

16 When the wind goes over it | it is | gone:
     and its | place will | know it · no | more.

17 But the merciful goodness of the Lord *
     endures for ever and ever toward | those that | fear him:
     and his righteousness up|on their | children's | children;

18 Upon those who | keep his | covenant:
     and | remember · his com|mandments · to | do them.

19 The Lord has established his | throne in | heaven:
     and his | kingdom | rules · over | all.

20 Praise the Lord all you his angels * you that ex|cel in | strength:
     you that fulfil his word * and obey the | voice of | his com|mandment.

21 Praise the Lord all | you his | hosts:
     his | servants · who | do his | will.

22 Praise the Lord all his works * in all places of | his do|minion:
     praise the | Lord | O my | soul!

104

WILLIAM RUSSELL

1 Bless the Lord | O my | soul:
    O Lord my | God how | great you | are!

2 Clothed with | majesty · and | honour:
    wrapped in | light as | in a | garment.

3 You have stretched out the | heavens · like a | tent-cloth:
    and laid the beams of your | dwelling · up|on their | waters;

4 You make the | clouds your | chariot:
    and | ride up·on the | wings · of the | wind;

5 You make the | winds your | messengers:
    and | flames of | fire your | ministers;

6 You have set the earth on | its found|ations:
    so | that it · shall | never · be | moved.

continued

7 The deep covered it ˈ as · with a ˈ mantle:
the waters ˈ stood aˈbove the ˈ hills.

8 At your reˈbuke they ˈ fled:
at the voice of your ˈ thunder · they ˈ hurried · aˈway;

9 They went up to the mountains * they went ˈ down · by the ˈ valleys:
to the place which ˈ you · had apˈpointed ˈ for them.

10 You fixed a limit which they ˈ may not ˈ pass:
they shall not return aˈgain to ˈ cover · the ˈ earth.

11 You send springs ˈ into · the ˈ gullies:
which ˈ run beˈtween the ˈ hills;

12 They give drink to every ˈ beast · of the ˈ field:
and the wild ˈ asses ˈ quench their ˈ thirst.

13 Beside them the birds of the air ˈ build their ˈ nests:
and ˈ sing aˈmong the ˈ branches.

14 You water the mountains from your ˈ dwelling · on ˈ high:
and the earth is ˈ filled · by the ˈ fruits of · your ˈ work.

15 You cause the grass to ˈ grow · for the ˈ cattle:
and all green things for the ˈ servants ˈ of manˈkind.

16 You bring food ˈ out of · the ˈ earth:
and wine that makes ˈ glad the ˈ heart of ˈ man,

17 Oil to give him a ˈ shining ˈ countenance:
and ˈ bread to ˈ strengthen · his ˈ heart.

18 The trees of the Lord are ˈ well-ˈwatered:
the cedars of ˈ Lebanon · that ˈ he has ˈ planted,

19 Where the birds ˈ build their ˈ nests:
and the stork ˈ makes her ˈ home · in the ˈ pine-tops.

20 The high hills are a refuge for the ˈ wild ˈ goats:
and the crags a ˈ cover ˈ for the ˈ conies.

21 You created the moon to ˈ mark the ˈ seasons:
and the sun ˈ knows the ˈ hour · of its ˈ setting.

22 You make darkness ˈ and it · is ˈ night:
in which all the beasts of the ˈ forest ˈ move by ˈ stealth.

23 The lions ˈ roar · for their ˈ prey:
  seekˈing their ˈ food from ˈ God.

24 When the sun rises ˈ they reˈtire:
  and ˈ lay them·selves ˈ down · in their ˈ dens.

† 25 Man goes ˈ out · to his ˈ work:
  and to his ˈ labour · unˈtil the ˈ evening.

180   THOMAS A. WALMISLEY

26 Lord how various ˈ are your ˈ works:
  in wisdom you have made them all * and the ˈ earth is ˈ full of · your ˈ creatures.

27 There is the wide imˈmeasur·able ˈ sea:
  there move living things without ˈ number ˈ great and ˈ small;

28 There go the ships ˈ to and ˈ fro:
  and there is that Leviathan * whom you ˈ formed to ˈ sport · in the ˈ deep.

29 These all ˈ look to ˈ you:
  to give them their ˈ food in ˈ due ˈ season.

30 When you give it to ˈ them they ˈ gather it:
  when you open your hand they are ˈ satisfied · with ˈ good ˈ things.

31 When you hide your ˈ face · they are ˈ troubled:
  when you take away their breath they ˈ die · and reˈturn · to their ˈ dust.

† 32 When you send forth your spirit they ˈ are creˈated:
  and you reˈnew the ˈ face · of the ˈ earth.

33 May the glory of the Lord enˈdure for ˈ ever:
  may the ˈ Lord reˈjoice · in his ˈ works.

34 If he look upon the ˈ earth · it shall ˈ tremble:
  if he but touch the ˈ mountains ˈ they shall ˈ smoke.

35 I will sing to the Lord as ˈ long as · I ˈ live:
  I will praise my ˈ God · while I ˈ have · any ˈ being.

36 May my meditation be ˈ pleasing ˈ to him:
  for my ˈ joy shall ˈ be · in the ˈ Lord.

† 37 May sinners perish from the earth * let the wicked ˈ be no ˈ more:
  bless the Lord O my soul * O ˈ praise ˈ — the ˈ Lord.

105

GEORGE J. ELVEY

1 O give thanks to the Lord   and call up|on his | name:
  tell among the | peoples · what | things · he has | done.

2 Sing to him O | sing | praises:
  and be telling of | all his | marvel·lous | works.

3 Exult in his | holy | name:
  and let those that seek the | Lord be | joyful · in | heart.

4 Seek the | Lord · and his | strength:
  O | seek his | face con|tinually.

5 Call to mind what wonders | he has | done:
  his marvellous acts   and the | judgements | of his | mouth,

6 O seed of | Abraham · his | servant:
  O | children · of | Jacob · his | chosen one.

7 For he is the | Lord our | God:
  and his judgements | are in | all the | earth.

8 He has remembered his | covenant · for | ever:
  the word that he ordained for a | thousand | gener|ations,

9 The covenant that he | made with | Abraham:
  the | oath · that he | swore to | Isaac,

10 And confirmed it to | Jacob · as a | statute:
   to Israel as an | ever|lasting | covenant,

† 11 Saying   'I will give you the | land of | Canaan:
   to be the | portion · of | your in|heritance.'

106

HENRY LAWES

1 Praise the Lord * O give thanks to the Lord for | he is | good:
and his | mercy · en|dures for | ever.

2 Who can express the mighty | acts · of the | Lord:
or | fully | voice his | praise?

3 Blessèd are those who act ac|cording · to | justice:
who at | all times | do the | right.

4 Remember me O Lord * when you visit your people | with your | favour:
and come to me | also · with | your sal|vation,

† 5 That I may see the prosperity | of your | chosen:
that I may rejoice with the rejoicing of your people *
and exult with | those who | are your | own.

6 We have sinned | like our | fathers:
we have acted per|versely · and | done | wrong.

7 Our fathers when they | were in | Egypt:
took no | heed | of your | wonders;

8 They did not remember the multitude of your | loving-|kindnesses:
but they re|belled · at the | Red | Sea.

9 Nevertheless he saved them for his | name's | sake:
that he | might make | known his | power.

10 He commanded the Red Sea and it | dried | up:
and he led them through the | deep as | through a | desert.

11 He delivered them from the | hand · of their | adversary;
and redeemed them | from the | power · of the | enemy.

12 The waters closed over | their op|pressors:
so that not | one was | left a|live.

13 Then they be|lieved his | words:
and | sang him | songs of | praise.

14 But in a little while they forgot what | he had | done:
and would | wait · for his | counsel · no | more.

15 Greed took hold of them | in the | desert:
and they put | God · to the | test · in the | wilderness.

continued

HENRY LAWES

42 Then was the wrath of the Lord kindled a⎪gainst his ⎪ people:
    and he ⎪ loathed his ⎪ own pos⎪session;

43 He gave them into the ⎪ hands · of the ⎪ nations:
    and their ⎪ adver·saries ⎪ ruled ⎪ over them.

44 Their enemies be⎪came · their op⎪pressors:
    and they were brought into sub⎪jection · be⎪neath their ⎪ power.

45 Many a ⎪ time he ⎪ saved them:
    but they rebelled against him to follow their own designs *
    and were brought ⎪ down ⎪ by their ⎪ wickedness.

46 Nevertheless he looked on ⎪ their dis⎪tress:
    when he ⎪ heard their ⎪ loud ⎪ crying.

47 He remembered his ⎪ coven·ant ⎪ with them:
    and relented   according to the a⎪bundance · of his ⎪ loving-⎪kindness.

48 And he caused them ⎪ to be ⎪ pitied:
    even by ⎪ those that ⎪ held them ⎪ captive.

49 Save us O Lord our God * and gather us from a⎪mong the ⎪ nations:
    that we may give thanks to your holy name *
    and ⎪ make our ⎪ boast · in your ⎪ praises.

† (50 Blessèd be the Lord the God of Israel * from everlasting to ⎪ ever⎪lasting:
    and let all the people say Amen * ⎪ Praise ⎪ — the ⎪ Lord.)

107

WALTER PARRATT

1 O give thanks to the Lord for ⎪ he is ⎪ good:
    for his loving ⎪ mercy ⎪ is for ⎪ ever.

2 Let the Lord's re⎪deemed ⎪ say so:
    whom he has redeemed from the ⎪ hand ⎪ of the ⎪ enemy,

† 3 And gathered in from every land * from the east and ⎪ from the ⎪ west:
    from the ⎪ north and ⎪ from the ⎪ south.

WALTER PARRATT

4 Some went astray in the wilderness and | in the | desert:
    and found no | path to · an in|habit·ed | city;

5 They were | hungry · and | thirsty:
    and their | heart | fainted · with|in them.

6 Then they cried to the Lord in | their dis|tress:
    and he | took them | out of · their | trouble.

7 He led them by the | right | path:
    till they | came to · an in|habit·ed | city.

UNISON   8 *Let them thank the | Lord · for his | goodness:*
    and for the wonders that he | does · for the | children · of | men;

UNISON   9 *For he | satisfies · the | thirsty:*
    and fills the | hungry · with | good | things.

10 Some sat in darkness and in | deadly | shadow:
    bound | fast · in af|fliction · and | iron,

11 Because they had rebelled against the | words of | God:
    and scorned the purposes | of the | Most | High.

12 So he bowed down their | hearts · with af|fliction:
    they tripped | headlong · with | none to | help them.

13 Then they cried to the Lord in | their dis|tress:
    and he | took them | out of · their | trouble.

†14 He brought them out from darkness and | deadly | shadow:
    and | broke their | chains in | two.

UNISON   15 *Let them thank the | Lord · for his | goodness:*
    and for the wonders that he | does · for the | children · of | men;

UNISON   16 *For he shatters the | doors of | bronze:*
    and | cleaves the | bars of | iron.

17 Fools were far | gone · in trans|gression:
    and be|cause of · their | sins · were af|flicted.

18 They sickened at | any | food:
    and had | come · to the | gates of | death.

19 Then they cried to the Lord in | their dis|tress:
    and he | took them | out of · their | trouble.   *continued*

20 He sent his ˈ word and ˈ healed them:
     and ˈ saved their ˈ life · from the ˈ Pit.

UNISON   21 *Let them thank the ˈ Lord · for his ˈ goodness:*
     and for the wonders that he ˈ does · for the ˈ children · of ˈ men;

UNISON   22 *Let them offer sacrifices of ˈ thanksˈgiving:*
     and tell what he has ˈ done with ˈ shouts of ˈ joy.

23 Those who go down to the ˈ sea in ˈ ships:
     and follow their ˈ trade on ˈ great ˈ waters,

24 These men have seen the ˈ works of ˈ God:
     and his ˈ wonders ˈ in the ˈ deep.

25 For he spoke and ˈ raised the ˈ storm-wind:
     and it lifted ˈ high the ˈ waves · of the ˈ sea.

26 They go up to the sky   and down aˈgain · to the ˈ depths:
     their courage melts aˈway · in the ˈ face · of disˈaster.

27 They reel and stagger like ˈ drunken ˈ men;
     and are ˈ at their ˈ wits' ˈ end.

28 Then they cried to the Lord in ˈ their disˈtress:
     and he ˈ took them ˈ out of · their ˈ trouble.

29 He calmed the ˈ storm · to a ˈ silence:
     and the ˈ waves · of the ˈ sea were ˈ stilled.

30 Then they were glad beˈcause · they were ˈ quiet:
     and he ˈ brought them · to the ˈ haven · they ˈ longed for.

UNISON   31 *Let them thank the ˈ Lord · for his ˈ goodness:*
     and for the wonders that he ˈ does · for the ˈ children · of ˈ men;

UNISON   32 *Let them exalt him in the asˈsembly · of the ˈ people:*
     and ˈ praise him · in the ˈcouncil · of ˈ elders.

108

184   ROBERT P. STEWART

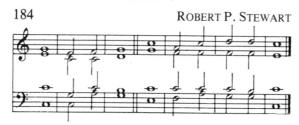

1 My heart is fixed O God my ǀ heart is ǀ fixed:
     I will ǀ sing and ǀ make ǀ melody.

2 Awake my soul   awake ǀ lute and ǀ harp:
     for ǀ I · will aǀwaken · the ǀ morning.

3 I will give you thanks O Lord aǀmong the ǀ peoples:
     I will sing your ǀ praise aǀmong the ǀ nations.

4 For the greatness of your mercy ǀ reaches · to the ǀ heavens:
     and your ǀ faithful·ness ǀ to the ǀ clouds.

5 Be exalted O God aǀbove the ǀ heavens:
     and let your glory be ǀ over ǀ all the ǀ earth;

6 That those whom you love may ǀ be deǀlivered:
     O save us by ǀ your right ǀ hand and ǀ answer me.

7 God has said in his ǀ holy ǀ place:
     'I will exult and divide Shechem * I will parcel ǀ out the ǀ valley · of ǀ Succoth.

8 'Gilead is mine and Manǀasseh · is ǀ mine:
     Ephraim is my helmet and ǀ Judah · my ǀ rod · of comǀmand.

† 9 'Moab is my wash-bowl   over Edom will I ǀ cast my ǀ shoe:
     against Philistia ǀ will I ǀ shout in ǀ triumph.'

10 Who will lead me into the ǀ forti·fied ǀ city:
     who will ǀ bring me ǀ into ǀ Edom?

11 Have you not cast us ǀ off O ǀ God?:
     you ǀ go not ǀ out · with our ǀ armies.

12 Give us your help aǀgainst the ǀ enemy:
     for ǀ vain · is the ǀ help of ǀ man.

13 By the power of our God we ǀ shall do ǀ valiantly:
     for it is he that ǀ will tread ǀ down our ǀ enemies.

110

JOHN DAVY

1 The Lord ǀ said to ǀ my lord:
   'Sit at my right hand * until I ǀ make your ǀ enemies · your ǀ footstool.'

2 The Lord commits to you the sceptre ǀ of your ǀ power:
   reign from ǀ Zion · in the ǀ midst of · your ǀ enemies.

3 Noble are you * from the day of your birth upon the ǀ holy ǀ hill:
   radiant are you even from the womb * in the ǀ morning ǀ dew of · your ǀ youth.

4 The Lord has sworn and will ǀ not turn ǀ back:
   'You are a priest for ever * after the ǀ order ǀ of Melǀchizedek.'

5 The king shall stand at your right ǀ hand O ǀ Lord:
   and shatter ǀ kings · in the ǀ day of · his ǀ wrath.

6 Glorious in majesty * he shall judge aǀmong the ǀ nations:
   and shatter heads ǀ over · a ǀ wide ǀ land.

† 7 He shall slake his thirst from the brook beǀside the ǀ way:
   therefore shall ǀ he lift ǀ up his ǀ head.

111

HENRY T. SMART

1 O praise the Lord * I will praise the Lord with my ǀ whole ǀ heart:
   in the company of the upright * and aǀmong the ǀ congreǀgation.

2 The works of the ǀ Lord are ǀ great:
   and studied by ǀ all who ǀ take deǀlight in them.

3 His deeds are maǀjestic · and ǀ glorious:
   and his ǀ righteous·ness ǀ stands for ǀ ever.

4 His marvellous acts have won him a name to ˈ be reˈmembered:
   the ˈ Lord is ˈ gracious · and ˈ merciful.

5 He gives food to ˈ those that ˈ fear him:
   he reˈmembers · his ˈ covenant · for ˈ ever.

6 He showed his people the ˈ power · of his ˈ acts:
   in giving them the ˈ herit·age ˈ of the ˈ heathen.

7 The works of his hands are ˈ faithful · and ˈ just:
   and ˈ all · his comˈmandments · are ˈ sure;

8 They stand firm for ˈ ever · and ˈ ever:
   they are done in ˈ faithful·ness ˈ and in ˈ truth.

9 He sent redemption to his people * he ordained his ˈ covenant · for ˈ ever:
   holy is his name and ˈ worthy ˈ to be ˈ feared.

10 The fear of the Lord is the beginning of wisdom *
   and of good understanding are those that ˈ keep · his comˈmandments:
   his ˈ praise · shall enˈdure for ˈ ever.

112

187   JOHN RANDALL

1 O praise the Lord * Blessèd is the man who ˈ fears the ˈ Lord:
   and greatly deˈlights in ˈ his comˈmandments.

2 His children shall be ˈ mighty · in the ˈ land:
   a race of upright ˈ men who ˈ will be ˈ blessed.ˈ

3 Riches and plenty shall be ˈ in his ˈ house:
   and his ˈ righteous·ness ˈ stands for ˈ ever.

4 Light arises in darkness ˈ for the ˈ upright:
   gracious and merciful ˈ is the ˈ righteous ˈ man.

5 It goes well with the man who acts ˈ generously · and ˈ lends:
   who ˈ guides · his afˈfairs with ˈ justice.

6 Surely he shall ˈ never · be ˈ moved:
   the righteous shall be held in ˈ everˈlasting · reˈmembrance.

7 He will not ˈ fear bad ˈ tidings:
   his heart is steadfast   ˈ trusting ˈ in the ˈ Lord.

8 His heart is confident and ˈ will not ˈ fear:
   he will see the ˈ downfall ˈ of his ˈ enemies.

continued

9 He gives ǀ freely · to the ǀ poor:
   his righteousness stands for ever * his ǀ head is · upǀlifted · in ǀ glory.

10 The wicked man shall see it ǀ and be ǀ angry:
   he shall gnash his teeth and consume away *
   and the ǀ hope · of the ǀ wicked · shall ǀ fail.

113

188   FREDERICK A. G. OUSELEY

1 Praise the Lord * O sing praises you that ǀ are his ǀ servants:
   O ǀ praise the ǀ name · of the ǀ Lord.

2 Let the name of the ǀ Lord be ǀ blessed:
   from this time ǀ forward ǀ and for ǀ ever.

3 From the rising of the sun to its ǀ going ǀ down:
   let the ǀ name · of the ǀ Lord be ǀ praised.

4 The Lord is exalted over ǀ all the ǀ nations:
   and his ǀ glory · is aǀbove the ǀ heavens.

5 Who can be likened to the ǀ Lord our ǀ God:
   in ǀ heaven · or upǀon the ǀ earth,

6 Who has his ǀ dwelling · so ǀ high:
   yet condescends to ǀ look on ǀ things beǀneath?

7 He raises the ǀ lowly · from the ǀ dust:
   and lifts the ǀ poor from ǀ out of · the ǀ dungheap;

8 He gives them a place aǀmong the ǀ princes:
   even among the ǀ princes ǀ of his ǀ people.

9 He causes the barren woman to ǀ keep ǀ house:
   and makes her a joyful mother of children * ǀ Praise ǀ — the ǀ Lord.

114

189

TONUS PEREGRINUS

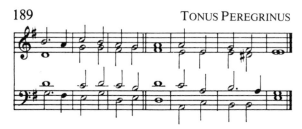

1 When Israel came ˈ out of ˈ Egypt:
  and the house of Jacob from among a ˈ people · of an ˈ alien ˈ tongue,

2 Judah beˈcame his ˈ sanctuary:
  and ˈ Israel ˈ his doˈminion.

3 The sea saw ˈ that and ˈ fled:
  Jorˈdan was ˈ driven ˈ back.

4 The mountains ˈ skipped like ˈ rams:
  and the little ˈ hills like ˈ young ˈ sheep.

5 What ailed you O ˈ sea · that you ˈ fled:
  O Jordan that ˈ you were ˈ driven ˈ back?

6 You mountains that you ˈ skipped like ˈ rams:
  and you little ˈ hills like ˈ young ˈ sheep?

7 Tremble O earth at the ˈ presence · of the ˈ Lord:
  at the ˈ presence · of the ˈ God of ˈ Jacob,

8 Who turned the rock into a ˈ pool of ˈ water:
  and the flint-stone ˈ into · a ˈ welling ˈ spring.

115

CHARLES F. SOUTH

1 Not to us O Lord not to us * but to your name | give the | glory:
   for the sake of your faithfulness | and your | loving-|kindness.

2 Why should the heathen say | 'Where is · their | God?':
   our God is in heaven   he | does what|ever · he | wills.

3 As for their idols   they are | silver · and | gold:
   the | work · of a | man's | hand.

4 They have | mouths but | speak not:
   they have | eyes · but they | cannot | see.

5 They have ears yet | hear | nothing:
   they have | noses · but | cannot | smell.

6 Hands they have but handle nothing * feet but they | do not | walk:
   they | make no | sound · with their | throats.

†7 Those who make them | shall be | like them:
   so shall | everyone · that | trusts in | them.

8 O Israel | trust · in the | Lord:
   he is your | help | and your | shield.

9 O house of Aaron | trust · in the | Lord:
   he is your | help | and your | shield.

10 You that fear the Lord | trust · in the | Lord:
   he is your | help | and your | shield.

11 The Lord has remembered us and | he will | bless us:
   he will bless the house of Israel * he will | bless the | house of | Aaron.

12 He will bless all those that | fear the | Lord:
   both | high and | low to|gether.

13 May the Lord in|crease you | greatly:
   you | and your | children | after you.

14 The blessing of the | Lord · be up|on you:
   he that | made | heaven · and | earth.

15 As for the heavens | they · are the | Lord's:
   but the earth he has | given · to the | children · of | men.

16 The dead do not | praise the | Lord:
        nor do | any · that go | down to | silence.

17 But we will | bless the | Lord:
        both now and for evermore * O | praise | — the | Lord.

116

RICHARD MASSEY

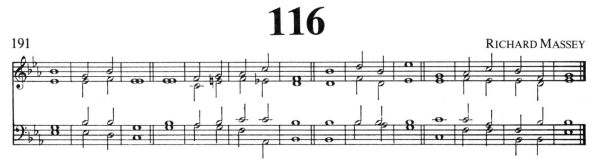

1   I love the Lord because he | heard my | voice:
        the | voice of · my | suppli|cation;

2   Because he in|clined his | ear to me:
        in the | day | that I | called to him.

3   The cords of death encompassed me * the snares of the | grave took | hold on me:
        I | was in | anguish · and | sorrow.

4   Then I called upon the | name of · the | Lord:
        'O | Lord · I be|seech you · de|liver me!'

5   Gracious and righteous | is the | Lord:
        full of com|passion | is our | God.

6   The Lord pre|serves the | simple:
        when | I was · brought | low he | saved me.

7   Return O my | soul · to your | rest:
        for the | Lord | has re|warded you.

8   For you O Lord have delivered my | soul from | death:
        my eyes from | tears · and my | feet from | falling.

† 9   I will walk be|fore the | Lord:
        in the | land | of the | living.

10 I believed that I would perish   I was | brought · very | low:
        I said in my haste | 'All | men are | liars.'

11 How shall I re|pay the | Lord:
        for | all his | bene·fits | to me?

12 I will take up the | cup of · sal|vation:
        and | call up·on the | name · of the | Lord.

continued

191   RICHARD MASSEY

13   I will pay my ˈ vows · to the ˈ Lord:
in the ˈ presence · of ˈ all his ˈ people.

14   Grievous in the ˈ sight · of the ˈ Lord:
is the ˈ death ˈ of his ˈ faithful ones.

15   O Lord I am your servant * your servant and the ˈ son of · your ˈ handmaid:
you ˈ have unˈloosed my ˈ bonds.

16   I will offer you a sacrifice of ˈ thanksˈgiving:
and ˈ call up·on the ˈ name · of the ˈ Lord.

17   I will pay my ˈ vows · to the ˈ Lord:
in the ˈ presence · of ˈ all his ˈ people,

† 18   In the courts of the ˈ house · of the ˈ Lord:
even in your midst O Jerusalem * ˈ Praise ˈ — the ˈ Lord.

117

192   JOHN STAINER

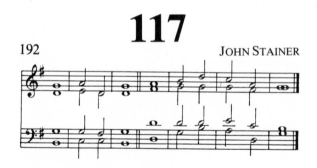

1   O praise the Lord ˈ all you ˈ nations:
O ˈ praise him ˈ all you ˈ peoples.

2   For great is his loving-ˈkindness · toˈward us:
and the faithfulness of the Lord endures for ever * ˈ Praise ˈ — the ˈ Lord.

118

GEORGE THALBEN-BALL

1 O give thanks to the Lord for ǀ he is ǀ good:
his ǀ mercy · enǀdures for ǀ ever.

2 Let Israel ǀ now proǀclaim:
that his ǀ mercy · enǀdures for ǀ ever.

3 Let the house of ǀ Aaron · proǀclaim:
that his ǀ mercy · enǀdures for ǀ ever.

4 Let those who fear the ǀ Lord proǀclaim:
that his ǀ mercy · enǀdures for ǀ ever.

5 In my danger I ǀ called · to the ǀ Lord:
he ǀ answered · and ǀ set me ǀ free.

6 The Lord is on my side   I ǀ shall not ǀ fear:
what can ǀ man ǀ do to ǀ me?

7 The Lord is at my side ǀ as my ǀ helper:
I shall see the ǀ downfall ǀ of my ǀ enemies.

8 It is better to take refuge ǀ in the ǀ Lord:
than to ǀ put your ǀ trust in ǀ man;

† 9 It is better to take refuge ǀ in the ǀ Lord:
than to ǀ put your ǀ trust in ǀ princes.

10 All the ǀ nations · surǀrounded me:
but in the name of the ǀ Lord I ǀ drove them ǀ back.

11 They surrounded   they surrounded me on ǀ every ǀ side:
but in the name of the ǀ Lord I ǀ drove them ǀ back.

12 They swarmed about me like bees * they blazed like fire aǀmong the ǀ thorns:
in the name of the ǀ Lord I ǀ drove them ǀ back.

13 I was pressed so hard that I ǀ almost ǀ fell:
but the ǀ Lord ǀ was my ǀ helper.

† 14 The Lord is my ǀ strength · and my ǀ song:
and has beǀcome ǀ my salǀvation.

15 The sounds of ǀ joy · and deǀliverance:
are ǀ in the ǀ tents · of the ǀ righteous.

16 The right hand of the Lord does ǀ mighty ǀ things:
the right hand of the ǀ Lord ǀ raises ǀ up.

continued

193

17 I shall not | die but | live:
    and pro|claim the | works · of the | Lord.

18 The Lord has | disciplined · me | hard:
    but he has not | given · me | over · to | death.

194

19 Open me the | gates of | righteousness:
    and I will enter and give | thanks | to the | Lord.

20 This is the | gate · of the | Lord:
    the | righteous | shall | enter it.

21 I will praise you | for you | answered me:
    and have be|come | my sal|vation.

22 The stone that the | builders · re|jected:
    has be|come the | head · of the | corner.

23 This is the | Lord's | doing:
    and it is | marvel·lous | in our | eyes.

24 This is the day that the | Lord has | made:
    let us re|joice | and be | glad in it.

25 O Lord | save us · we | pray:
    O Lord | send | us pros|perity.

26 Blessèd is he who comes in the | name · of the | Lord:
    from the | house · of the | Lord we | bless you.

27 The Lord is God   and he has | given · us | light:
    guide the festal throng up to the | horns | of the | altar.

28 You are my God and | I will | praise you:
    you are my | God I | will ex|alt you.

† 29 O give thanks to the Lord for | he is | good:
    and his | mercy · en|dures for | ever.

119(1)

HENRY ALDRICH

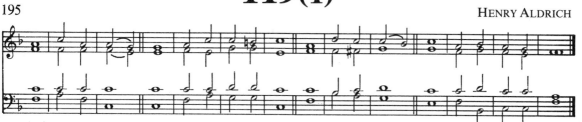

1   Blessèd are those whose | way is | blameless:
     who | walk · in the | law · of the | Lord.

2   Blessèd are those who | keep · his com|mands:
     and seek him | with their | whole | heart;

3   Those who | do no | wrong:
     but | walk · in the | ways of · our | God.

4   For you Lord | have com|manded us:
     to perse|vere in | all your | precepts.

5   If only my | ways · were un|erring:
     towards the | keeping | of your | statutes!

6   Then I should | not · be a|shamed:
     when I | looked on | all · your com|mandments.

7   I will praise you with sin|cerity · of | heart:
     as I | learn your | righteous | judgements.

8   I will | keep your | statutes:
     O for|sake me | not | utterly.

119(2)

STEPHEN ELVEY

196

9   How shall a young man's | path be | pure:
        un|less he | keep to · your | word?

10   I have sought you with my | whole | heart:
        let me not | stray from | your com|mandments.

11   I have treasured your | words · in my | heart:
        that I | might not | sin a|gainst you.

12   Blessèd are | you Lord | God:
        O | teach me | your | statutes.

13   With my lips I | have been | telling:
        all the | judgements | of your | mouth;

14   And I find more joy in the way of | your com|mands:
        than in | all | manner · of | riches.

15   I will meditate | on your | precepts:
        and give | heed | to your | ways;

16   For my delight is wholly | in your | statutes:
        and I will | not for|get your | word.

119(3)

WILLIAM RUSSELL

197

17   O be bountiful to your servant that | I may | live:
        in o|bedi·ence | to your | word.

18   Take away the | veil · from my | eyes:
        that I may see the | wonders | of your | law.

19 I am but a | stranger · on the | earth:
  do not | hide · your com|mandments | from me.

20 My soul is con|sumed with | longing:
  for your | judgements | day and | night.

21 You have re|buked the | proud:
  and cursed are those who | stray from | your com|mandments;

22 Turn away from me their re|proach and | scorn:
  for | I have | kept · your com|mands.

23 Though princes sit and plot to|gether · a|gainst me:
  your servant shall | medi·tate | on your | statutes:

24 For your commands are | my de|light:
  and they are | counsellors · in | my de|fence.

119(4)

198

JOHN GOSS

25 I am humbled | to the | dust:
  O give me life ac|cording | to your | word.

26 If I ex|amine · my | ways:
  surely you will answer me * O | teach me | your | statutes!

27 Make me to understand the | way of · your | precepts;
  and I shall meditate | on your | marvel·lous | works.

28 My soul pines a|way for | sorrow:
  O raise me up ac|cording | to your | word.

29 Keep me far from the | way of · de|ception:
  and | grant me · the | grace of · your | law.

30 I have chosen the | way of | truth:
  and have | set your | judgements · be|fore me.

31 I hold fast to | your com|mands:
  O Lord let me | never | be con|founded.

32 Let me run the way of | your com|mandments:
  for | you will | liberate · my | heart.

119(5)

THOMAS HANFORTH

199

33 Teach me O Lord the | way of · your | statutes:
  and I will | honour · it | to the | end.

34 Give me understanding   that I may | keep your | law:
  that I may keep it | with my | whole | heart.

35 Guide me in the path of | your com|mandments:
  for there|in is | my de|light.

36 Incline my heart to | your com|mands:
  and | not to | selfish | gain.

37 Turn away my eyes from | looking · on | vanities:
  as I walk in your | way | give me | life.

38 Make good your promise | to your | servant:
  the promise that en|dures for | all who | fear you.

39 Turn aside the | taunts · that I | dread:
  for your | judgements · are | very | good.

40 Lord I | long for · your | precepts:
  in your | righteous·ness | give me | life.

119(6)

EDMUND CHIPP

200

41 Let your loving mercy come to | me O | Lord:
  and your salvation ac|cording | to your | word.

42 Then I shall have an answer for | those · who re|proach me:
  for I | trust | in your | word.

43 Do not take the word of truth utterly ǀ out of · my ǀ mouth:
for in your ǀ judgements ǀ is my ǀ hope.

44 Let me keep your ǀ law conǀtinually:
O ǀ let me ǀ keep it · for ǀ ever.

45 And so I shall ǀ walk at ǀ liberty:
beǀcause · I have ǀ sought your ǀ precepts.

46 I shall speak of your comǀmands be·fore ǀ kings:
and shall ǀ not be ǀ put to ǀ shame.

47 My delight shall be in ǀ your comǀmandments;
which ǀ I have ǀ greatly ǀ loved;

48 I shall worship you with ǀ outstretched ǀ hands:
and I shall ǀ medi·tate ǀ on your ǀ statutes.

119(7)

HEZEKIAH WEST

201

49 Remember your ǀ word · to your ǀ servant:
on ǀ which · you have ǀ built my ǀ hope.

50 This has been my comfort in ǀ my afǀfliction:
for your ǀ word has ǀ brought me ǀ life.

51 Though the proud have ǀ laughed me · to ǀ scorn:
I have not ǀ turned aǀside from · your ǀ law;

52 But I called to·mind O Lord your ǀ judgements · of ǀ old:
and in ǀ them · I have ǀ found · consolǀation.

53 I am seized with indignation ǀ at the ǀ wicked:
for ǀ they have · forǀsaken · your ǀ law.

54 But your statutes have beǀcome my ǀ songs:
in the ǀ house ǀ of my ǀ pilgrimage.

55 I think on your name O ǀ Lord · in the ǀ night:
and ǀ I obǀserve your ǀ law;

56 This has ǀ been · my reǀward:
beǀcause · I have ǀ kept your ǀ precepts.

119(8)

S. S. WESLEY

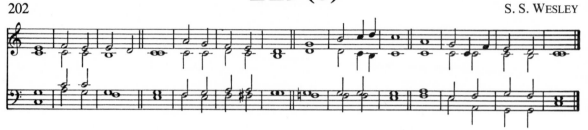

57 The Lord | is my | portion:
    I have | promised · to | keep your | words.

58 I have sought your favour with my | whole | heart:
    O be gracious to me ac|cording | to your | word.

59 I have taken | stock of · my | ways:
    and have turned back my | feet to | your com|mands.

60 I made haste and did | not de|lay:
    to | keep | your com|mandments.

61 The snares of the | wicked · en|compassed me:
    but I did | not for|get your | law;

62 At midnight I rise to | give you | thanks:
    for the | righteous·ness | of your | judgements.

63 I am a friend to | all who | fear you:
    to | those who | keep your | precepts.

64 The earth O Lord is full of your | loving | mercy:
    O | teach me | your | statutes.

119 (9)

S. S. WESLEY

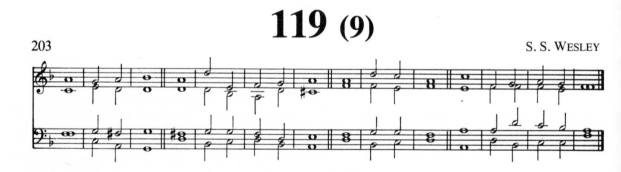

65 Lord you have done | good to · your | servant:
    in ac|cordance | with your | word.

66 O teach me right | judgement · and | knowledge:
    for I | trust in | your com|mandments.

67 Before I was afflicted I ' went a'stray:
   but ' now I ' keep your ' word.

68 You are good and you ' do ' good:
   O ' teach me ' your ' statutes.

69 The proud have ' smeared me · with ' lies:
   but I will keep your precepts ' with my ' whole ' heart.

70 Their hearts are ' gross like ' fat:
   but my de'light is ' in your ' law.

71 It is good for me that ' I was · af'flicted:
   so ' I might ' learn your ' statutes.

72 The law of your mouth is ' dearer · to ' me:
   than a ' wealth of ' gold and ' silver.

119(10)

S. MATTHEWS

73 Your hands have ' made me · and ' fashioned me:
   O give me understanding that ' I may ' learn · your com'mandments.

74 Those who fear you shall see me ' and re'joice:
   for my ' hope is ' in your ' word.

75 I know Lord that your ' judgements · are ' right:
   and that in ' faithfulness · you ' have af'flicted me.

76 Let your merciful kindness ' be my ' comfort:
   according to your ' promise ' to your ' servant.

77 O let your mercy come to me that ' I may ' live:
   for your ' law is ' my de'light.

78 Let the proud be shamed * who steal my ' rights · through their ' lies:
   but I will ' medi·tate ' on your ' precepts.

79 Let those who fear you ' turn to ' me:
   and ' they shall ' know · your com'mands.

80 O let my heart be ' sound in · your ' statutes:
   that I may ' never · be ' put to ' shame.

119(11)

T. Tertius Noble

81 My soul languishes for | your sal|vation:
   but my | hope is | in your | word;

82 My eyes fail with | watching · for your | promise:
   saying 'O | when | will you | comfort me?'

83 I am parched as a wineskin | in the | smoke:
   yet I do | not for|get your | statutes.

84 How many are the | days of · your | servant:
   and | when · will you | judge my | persecutors?

85 The proud have dug | pitfalls | for me:
   in de|fiance | of your | law.

86 All your com|mandments · are | true:
   but they persecute me with lies * O | come | to my | help!

87 They have almost made an end of me | on the | earth:
   but I have | not for|saken · your | precepts.

88 In your merciful goodness | give me | life:
   that I may keep the com|mands | of your | mouth.

119(12)

George Thalben-Ball

89 Lord your | word · is for | ever:
   it stands | firm | in the | heavens.

90 Your faithfulness abides from one gener|ation · to an|other:
   firm as the | earth which | you have | made.

91 As for your judgements   they stand | fast this | day:
for | all things | are your | servants.

92 If your law had not been | my de|light:
I would have | perished · in | my af|fliction.

93 I will never for|get your | precepts:
for by | them · you have | given · me | life.

94 I am | yours O | save me:
for | I have | sought your | precepts.

95 The wicked have lain in wait for me | to de|stroy me:
but I | think on | your com|mands.

96 I have seen that all perfection | comes · to an | end:
only your com|mandment | has no | bounds.

119(13)

207

J. L. ROGERS

97 Lord how I | love your | law:
it is my medi|tation | all the · day | long.

98 Your commandments have made me wiser | than my | enemies:
for they re|main with | me for | ever.

99 I have more understanding than | all my | teachers:
for I | study | your com|mands.

100 I am wiser | than the | agèd:
be|cause · I have | kept your | precepts.

101 I have held back my feet from every | evil | path:
that | I might | keep your | word;

102 I have not turned a|side from · your | judgements:
for | you your|self are · my | teacher.

103 How sweet are your | words · to my | tongue:
sweeter than | honey | to my | mouth.

104 Through your precepts I get | under|standing:
therefore I | hate all | lying | ways.

119(14)

JOHN CAMIDGE Junior

208

105 Your word is a lantern ǀ to my ǀ feet:
and a ǀ light ǀ to my ǀ path.

106 I have vowed and ǀ sworn an ǀ oath:
to ǀ keep your ǀ righteous ǀ judgements.

107 I have been afflicted beǀyond ǀ measure:
Lord give me life acǀcording ǀ to your ǀ word.

108 Accept O Lord the freewill offerings ǀ of my ǀ mouth:
and ǀ teach me ǀ your ǀ judgements.

109 I take my life in my ǀ hands conǀtinually:
yet I do ǀ not forǀget your ǀ law.

110 The wicked have ǀ laid a ǀ snare for me:
but I ǀ have not ǀ strayed from · your ǀ precepts.

111 Your commands are my inǀheritance · for ǀ ever:
they ǀ are the ǀ joy of · my ǀ heart.

112 I have set my heart to fulǀfil your ǀ statutes:
always ǀ even ǀ to the ǀ end.

119(15)

THOMAS ATTWOOD

209

113 I loathe those who are ǀ double-ǀminded:
but your ǀ law ǀ do I ǀ love.

114 You are my shelter ǀ and my ǀ shield:
and in your ǀ word ǀ is my ǀ hope.

115 Away from me all | you that · do | evil:
    I will keep the com|mandments | of my | God.

116 Be my stay according to your word that | I may | live:
    and do not disap|point me | in my | hope.

117 Hold me up and I | shall be | safe:
    and I will ever de|light | in your | statutes.

118 You scorn all those who | swerve from · your | statutes:
    for their | calumnies · a|gainst me · are | lies;

119 All the ungodly of the earth you | count as | dross:
    therefore I | love | your com|mands.

120 My flesh | shrinks for | fear of you:
    and I am a|fraid | of your | judgements.

119(16)

210

EDWARD HIGGINS

121 I have done what is | just and | right:
    O do not give me | over · to | my op|pressors.

122 Stand surety for your | servant's | good:
    let | not the | proud op|press me.

123 My eyes fail with watching for | your sal|vation:
    for the fulfilment | of your | righteous | word.

124 O deal with your servant according to your | loving mercy:
    and | teach me | your | statutes.

125 I am your servant   O give me | under|standing:
    that | I may | know · your com|mands.

126 It is time for the | Lord to | act:
    for they | viol·ate | your | law.

127 Therefore I | love · your com|mandments:
    more than gold | more · than the | finest | gold;

128 Therefore I straighten my paths by | all your | precepts:
    and I | hate all | lying | ways.

175

119(17)

RICHARD LANGDON

129 Wonderful are ˈ your comˈmands:
and ˈ therefore · my ˈ soul ˈ keeps them.

130 The unfolding of your ˈ word gives ˈ light:
it gives underˈstanding ˈ to the ˈ simple.

131 I open my mouth and draw ˈ in my ˈ breath:
for I ˈ yearn for ˈ your comˈmandments.

132 O turn to me and be ˈ merci · ful ˈ to me:
as is your way with ˈ those who ˈ love your ˈ name.

133 Order my steps according ˈ to your ˈ word:
that no evil ˈ may get ˈ master · y ˈ over me.

134 Deliver me from ˈ man's opˈpression:
that ˈ I may ˈ keep your ˈ precepts.

135 Make your face shine upˈon your ˈ servant:
and ˈ teach me ˈ your ˈ statutes.

136 My eyes gush out with ˈ streams of ˈ water:
because they ˈ pay no ˈ heed to · your ˈ law.

119(18)

S. S. WESLEY

137 Righteous are ˈ you Lord ˈ God:
and ˈ just are ˈ your ˈ judgements;

138 The commands that ˈ you · have comˈmanded:
are exˈceeding · ly ˈ righteous · and ˈ true.

139 Zeal and indignation have | choked my | mouth:
    because my enemies | have for|gotten · your | words.

140 Your word has been | tried · in the | fire:
    and | therefore · your | servant | loves it.

141 I am small and of | no ac|count:
    but I have | not for|gotten · your | precepts.

142 Your righteousness is an ever|lasting | righteousness:
    and your | law | is the | truth.

143 Trouble and anguish have | taken | hold on me:
    but your com|mandments · are | my de|light.

144 The righteousness of your commands is | ever|lasting:
    O give me under|standing · and | I shall | live.

119(19)

GEORGE C. MARTIN

213

145 I call with my | whole | heart:
    hear me O Lord | I will | keep your | statutes.

146 I cry out to | you O | save me:
    and | I will | heed · your com|mands.

147 Before the morning light I | rise · and I | call:
    for in your | word | is my | hope.

148 Before the night watch my | eyes | wake:
    that I may | meditate · up|on your | words.

149 Hear my voice O Lord in your | loving | mercy:
    and according to your | judgements | give me | life.

150 They draw near to me who mal|icious·ly | persecute me:
    but | they are | far from · your | law.

151 You Lord are | close at | hand:
    and | all · your com|mandments · are | true.

152 I have known long since from | your com|mands:
    that you have | founded | them for | ever.

119(20)

HIGHMORE SKEATS Junior

153 Consider my affliction | and de|liver me:
    for I do | not for|get your | law.

154 Plead my cause and | set me | free:
    O give me life ac|cording | to your | word.

155 Salvation is | far · from the | wicked:
    for they | do not | seek your | statutes.

156 Numberless O Lord are your | tender | mercies:
    according to your | judgements | give me | life.

157 Many there are that persecute | me and | trouble me:
    but I have not | swerved from | your com|mands.

158 I am cut to the heart when I | see the | faithless:
    for they | do not | keep your | word.

159 Consider O Lord how I | love your | precepts:
    and in your | mercy | give me | life.

160 The sum of your | word is | truth:
    and all your righteous | judgements | stand for | ever.

119(21)

GEORGE COOPER

161 Princes have persecuted me with|out a | cause:
    but my heart | stands in | awe of · your | word.

162 I am as | glad of · your | word:
    as | one who | finds rich | spoil.

163 Lies I | hate · and ab|hor:
      but your | law | do I | love.

164 Seven times a | day I | praise you:
      be|cause of · your | righteous | judgements.

165 Great is the peace of those who | love your | law:
      and | nothing · shall | make them | stumble.

166 Lord I have waited for | your sal|vation:
      and I have | done | your com|mandments.

167 My soul has heeded | your com|mands:
      and I | love them · be|yond | measure.

168 I have kept your precepts | and com|mands:
      for all my | ways are | open · be|fore you.

119(22)

216

JOHN JONES

169 Let my cry | come to you · O | Lord:
      O give me understanding ac|cording | to your | word;

170 Let my supplication | come be|fore you:
      and deliver me ac|cording | to your | promise.

171 My lips shall pour | forth your | praise:
      be|cause you | teach me · your | statutes;

172 My tongue shall | sing of · your | word:
      for | all · your com|mandments · are | righteousness.

173 Let your hand be | swift to | help me:
      for | I have | chosen · your | precepts.

174 Lord I have longed for | your sal|vation:
      and your | law is | my de|light.

175 O let my soul live that | I may | praise you:
      and let your | judgements | be my | help.

176 I have gone astray like a | sheep · that is | lost:
      O seek your servant * for I do | not for|get · your com|mandments.

121

JAMES TURLE

H. WALFORD DAVIES

1. I lift up my | eyes · to the | hills:
   but | where · shall I | find | help?

2. My help | comes · from the | Lord:
   who has | made | heaven · and | earth.

3. He will not suffer your | foot to | stumble:
   and he who watches | over · you | will not | sleep.

4. Be sure he who has | charge of | Israel:
   will | neither | slumber · nor | sleep.

5. The Lord him|self is · your | keeper:
   the Lord is your defence up|on your | right | hand;

6. The sun shall not | strike you · by | day:
   nor | shall the | moon by | night.

7. The Lord will defend you from | all | evil:
   it is | he · who will | guard your | life.

8. The Lord will defend your going out and your | coming | in:
   from this time | forward · for | ever|more.

122

JOHN ROBINSON

1   I was glad when they | said to | me:
     'Let us | go · to the | house · of the | Lord.'

2   And now our | feet are | standing:
     with|in your | gates · O Je|rusalem;

† 3   Jerusalem which is | built · as a | city:
     where the | pilgrims | gather · in | unity.

4   There the tribes go up   the | tribes · of the | Lord:
     as he commanded Israel * to give | thanks · to the | name · of the | Lord.

5   There are set | thrones of | judgement:
     the | thrones · of the | house of | David.

6   O pray for the | peace · of Je|rusalem:
     may | those who | love you | prosper.

7   Peace be with|in your | walls:
     and pros|peri·ty | in your | palaces.

8   For the sake of my brothers | and com|panions:
     I will | pray that | peace be | with you.

9   For the sake of the house of the | Lord our | God:
     I will | seek | for your | good.

123

ANONYMOUS

1 To you I lift | up my | eyes:
  you who are en|throned | in the | heavens.

2 As the eyes of servants look to the | hand of · their | master:
  or as the eyes of a maid to|ward the | hand of · her | mistress,

3 So our eyes look to the | Lord our | God:
  un|til he | show us · his | mercy.

4 Have mercy upon us O Lord have | mercy · up|on us:
  for we have | had our | fill · of de|rision.

5 Our souls overflow with the mockery of | those at | ease:
  and with the | contempt | of the | proud.

124

221

J. HARRISON

1 If the Lord had not been on our side * now may | Israel | say:
  if the Lord had not been on our side when | men rose | up a|gainst us,

2 Then they would have | swallowed us · a|live:
  when their | anger · was | kindled · a|gainst us.

3 Then the waters would have overwhelmed us * and the | torrent · gone | over us:
  the raging waters | would have | gone clean | over us.

J. Harrison

4 But praised | be the | Lord:
   who has not given us as a | prey | to their | teeth:

5 We have escaped like a bird from the | snare · of the | fowler:
   the snare is | broken · and | we have · gone | free.

6 Our help is in the | name · of the | Lord:
   who has | made | heaven · and | earth.

125

223   John Hindle

1 Those who put their trust in the Lord shall | be as · Mount | Zion:
   which cannot be | shaken · but en|dures for | ever.

2 As the mountains stand about Jerusalem * so stands the Lord a|bout his | people:
   from this time | forward · for | ever|more.

3 For the sceptre of wickedness shall have no sway *
   over the land apportioned | to the | righteous:
   lest the righteous | set their | hands to · do | evil.

4 Do good O Lord to | those · who are | good:
   to | those · that are | upright · in | heart.

5 As for those who turn aside to crooked ways *
   let the Lord lead them away with the | evil|doers:
   and in | Israel | let there · be | peace.

126

EDWARD CUTLER

1 When the Lord turned again the ǀ fortunes · of ǀ Zion:
   then were we like ǀ men reǀstored to ǀ life.

2 Then was our mouth ǀ filled with ǀ laughter:
   and ǀ our ǀ tongue with ǀ singing.

3 Then said they aǀmong the ǀ heathen:
   'The Lord has ǀ done great ǀ things for ǀ them.'

4 Truly the Lord has done great ǀ things for ǀ us:
   and ǀ therefore ǀ we reǀjoiced.

5 Turn again our ǀ fortunes · O ǀ Lord:
   as the streams reǀturn · to the ǀ dry ǀ south.

6 Those that ǀ sow in ǀ tears:
   shall ǀ reap with ǀ songs of ǀ joy.

† 7 He who goes out weeping   ǀ bearing · the ǀ seed:
   shall come again in gladness ǀ bringing · his ǀ sheaves ǀ with him.

127

JOHN STAINER

1 Unless the Lord ǀ builds the ǀ house:
   their labour ǀ is but ǀ lost that ǀ build it.

2 Unless the Lord ǀ keeps the ǀ city:
   the ǀ watchmen ǀ watch in ǀ vain.

3 It is in vain that you rise up early and go so late to rest * eating the ǀ bread of ǀ toil:
for the Lord bestows honour   ǀ and on ǀ those · whom he ǀ loves.

4 Behold   children are a heritage [|] from the [|] Lord:
   and the [|] fruit · of the [|] womb is · his [|] gift.

5 Like arrows in the [|] hand · of a [|] warrior:
   are the [|] sons · of a [|] man's [|] youth.

6 Happy the man who has his [|] quiver [|] full of them;
   he will not be put to shame * when he confronts his [|] enem · ies [|] at the [|] gate.

128

JOHN GOSS

1 Blessèd is everyone who [|] fears the [|] Lord:
   and walks in the [|] confine [|] of his [|] ways.

2 You will eat the [|] fruit of · your [|] labours:
   happy shall you [|] be and [|] all · shall go [|] well with you.

3 Your wife with[|]in your [|] house:
   shall [|] be · as a [|] fruitful [|] vine;

4 Your children a[|]round your [|] table:
   like the fresh [|] shoots [|] of the [|] olive.

5 Behold thus shall the [|] man be [|] blessed:
   who [|] lives · in the [|] fear · of the [|] Lord.

6 May the Lord so [|] bless you · from [|] Zion:
   that you see Jerusalem in prosperity [|] all the [|] days of · your [|] life.

† 7 May you see your [|] children's [|] children:
   and in [|] Israel [|] let there · be [|] peace.

130

from PURCELL

228   C. HYLTON STEWART

1 Out of the depths have I called to ˈ you O ˈ Lord:
   Lord ˈ hear ˈ my ˈ voice;

2 O let your ears conˈsider ˈ well:
   the ˈ voice · of my ˈ suppliˈcation.

3 If you Lord should note what ˈ we do ˈ wrong:
   who ˈ then O ˈ Lord could ˈ stand?

4 But there is forˈgiveness · with ˈ you:
   so that ˈ you ˈ shall be ˈ feared.

5 I wait for the Lord * my ˈ soul ˈ waits for him:
   and ˈ in his ˈ word · is my ˈ hope.

6 My soul ˈ looks · for the ˈ Lord:
   more than watchmen for the morning *
       more I say than ˈ watchmen ˈ for the ˈ morning.

7 O Israel trust in the Lord * for with the ˈ Lord · there is ˈ mercy:
   and with ˈ him is ˈ ample · reˈdemption.

8 He will reˈdeem ˈ Israel:
   from the ˈ multi·tude ˈ of his ˈ sins.

131

C. A. WICKES

1 O Lord my | heart is · not | proud:
   nor | are my | eyes | haughty.

2 I do not busy myself in | great | matters:
   or in | things too | wonder·ful | for me.

3 But I have calmed and quieted my soul *
   like a weaned child upon its | mother's | breast:
   like a child on its mother's breast | is my | soul with|in me.

4 O Israel | trust · in the | Lord:
   from this time | forward | and for | ever.

132

FREDERICK A. G. OUSELEY

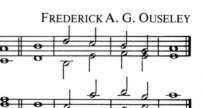

1 Lord remember David and | all his | trouble:
   how he swore an oath to the Lord * and vowed to the | Mighty | One of | Jacob;

2 'I will not enter the | shelter · of my | house:
   nor climb into the | comfort | of my | bed;

3 'I will not give | sleep to · my | eyes:
   or | slumber | to my | eyelids,

4 'Till I find out a place for the | ark · of the | Lord:
   a dwelling for the | Mighty | One of | Jacob.'

5 Lo we | heard of it · at | Ephrathah:
   we | found it · in the | fields of | Ja-ar.

6 Let us go to the | place of · his | dwelling:
   let us fall upon our | knees be|fore his | footstool.

7 Arise O Lord | into · your | resting-place:
   you | and the | ark of · your | might.

8 Let your priests be | clothed with | righteousness:
   and let your | faithful · ones | shout for | joy.

† 9 For the sake of | David · your | servant:
   do not turn away the | face of | your an|ointed.

10 The Lord has | sworn to | David:
   an | oath · which he | will not | break;

11 'One who is the | fruit of · your | body:
   I will | set up|on your | throne.

12 'If your children will keep my covenant * and the com|mands · which I | teach them:
   their children also shall sit up|on your | throne for | ever.'

13 For the Lord has chosen | Zion · for him|self:
   he has de|sired it · for his | habi|tation.

14 'This shall be my | resting-place · for | ever:
   here will I dwell   for | my de|light · is in | her.

15 'I will bless her pro|visions · with a|bundance:
   I will | satisfy · her | poor with | bread.

FREDERICK A. G. OUSELEY

16 'I will clothe her | priests with · sal|vation:
    and her | faithful ones · shall | shout for | joy.

17 'There will I make a horn to sprout for the | family · of | David:
    I have prepared a | lamp for | my an|ointed.

†18 'As for his enemies   I will | cover them · with | shame:
    but upon his | head · shall his | crown be | bright.'

133

231

VINCENT NOVELLO

1 Behold how good and how | lovely · it | is:
    when brothers | live to|gether · in | unity.

2 It is fragrant as oil upon the head * that runs down | over · the | beard:
    fragrant as oil upon the beard of Aaron *
    that ran down over the | collar | of his | robe.

3 It is like a | dew of | Hermon:
    like the dew that falls up|on the | hill of | Zion.

4 For there the Lord has com|manded · his | blessing:
    which is | life for | ever|more.

135

1 Praise the Lord * praise the | name · of the | Lord:
   praise him you | servants | of the | Lord,

2 Who stand in the | house · of the | Lord:
   in the | courts · of the | house of · our | God.

3 Praise the Lord for the | Lord is | gracious:
   sing praises to his | name for | it is | good.

4 For the Lord has chosen Jacob | for him|self:
   and Israel | as his | own pos|session.

5 I know that the | Lord is | great:
   and that our | Lord · is a|bove all | gods.

6 He does whatever he wills * in heaven and up|on the | earth:
   in the seas and | in the | great | depths.

7 He brings up clouds from the | ends · of the | earth:
   he makes lightning for the rain * and brings the | wind | out of · his | storehouses.

8 He struck down the | firstborn · of | Egypt:
   both | man and | beast a|like.

9 He sent signs and wonders into your | midst O | Egypt:
   against Pharaoh and a|gainst | all his | servants.

10 He struck down | great | nations:
   and | slew | mighty | kings,

11 Sihon king of the Amorites   and Og the | king of | Bashan:
   and | all the | princes · of | Canaan.

12 He made over their | land · as a | heritage:
   a | heritage · for | Israel · his | people.

13 O Lord your name shall en|dure for | ever:
   so shall your renown through|out all | gener|ations.

14 For the Lord will | vindicate · his | people:
   he will take | pity | on his | servants.

15 As for the idols of the nations * they are but | silver · and | gold:
   the | work · of a | man's | hand.

16 They have | mouths but | speak not:
   they have | eyes · but they | cannot | see.

17 They have ears yet | hear | nothing:
there is no | breath | in their | nostrils.

18 Those who make them | shall be | like them:
so shall | every|one that | trusts in them.

19 Bless the Lord O | house of | Israel:
bless the | Lord O | house of | Aaron.

20 Bless the Lord O | house of | Levi:
you that | fear the · Lord | bless the | Lord.

† 21 Blessèd be the | Lord from | Zion:
he that dwells in Jerusalem * | Praise | — the | Lord.

136

233

CHARLES H. LLOYD

omit in Gloria

1 O give thanks to the Lord for | he is | good:
for his | mercy · en|dures for | ever.

2 O give thanks to the | God of | gods:
for his | mercy · en|dures for | ever.

† 3 O give thanks to the | Lord of | lords:
for his | mercy · en|dures for | ever;

4 To him who alone does | great | wonders:
for his | mercy · en|dures for | ever;

5 Who by wisdom | made the | heavens:
for his | mercy · en|dures for | ever;

6 Who stretched out the earth up|on the | waters:
for his | mercy · en|dures for | ever;

7 Who made the | great | lights:
for his | mercy · en|dures for | ever;

8 The sun to | rule the | day:
for his | mercy · en|dures for | ever;

9 The moon and the stars to | govern · the | night:
for his | mercy · en|dures for | ever;

continued

CHARLES H. LLOYD

10 Who struck down Egypt ˡ and its ˡ firstborn:
    for his ˡ mercy · enˡdures for ˡ ever;

11 Who brought out Israel ˡ from aˡmong them:
    for his ˡ mercy · enˡdures for ˡ ever;

† 12 With a strong hand and with ˡ outstretched ˡ arm:
    for his ˡ mercy · enˡdures for ˡ ever;

13 Who divided the Red Sea into ˡ two ˡ parts:
    for his ˡ mercy · enˡdures for ˡ ever;

14 And made Israel pass ˡ through the ˡ midst of it:
    for his ˡ mercy · enˡdures for ˡ ever;

15 Who cast off Pharaoh and his host into the ˡ Red ˡ Sea:
    for his ˡ mercy · enˡdures for ˡ ever;

16 Who led his people ˡ through the ˡ wilderness:
    for his ˡ mercy · enˡdures for ˡ ever;

17 Who struck down ˡ great ˡ kings:
    for his ˡ mercy · enˡdures for ˡ ever;

18 Who slew ˡ mighty ˡ kings:
    for his ˡ mercy · enˡdures for ˡ ever;

19 Sihon ˡ king · of the ˡ Amorites:
    for his ˡ mercy · enˡdures for ˡ ever;

20 And Og the ˡ king of ˡ Bashan:
    for his ˡ mercy · enˡdures for ˡ ever;

21 Who made over their ˡ land · as a ˡ heritage:
    for his ˡ mercy · enˡdures for ˡ ever;

22 As a heritage for ˡ Israel · his ˡ servant:
    for his ˡ mercy · enˡdures for ˡ ever;

23 Who remembered us in our huˡmiliˡation:
    for his ˡ mercy · enˡdures for ˡ ever;

24 And delivered us ˡ from our ˡ enemies:
    for his ˡ mercy · enˡdures for ˡ ever;

25 Who gives food to ˡ all that ˡ lives:
    for his ˡ mercy · enˡdures for ˡ ever;

26 O give thanks to the ˡ God of ˡ heaven:
    for his ˡ mercy · enˡdures for ˡ ever.

137

CHARLES H. LLOYD

1   By the waters of Babylon we sat ˈ down and ˈ wept:
    when ˈ we reˈmembered ˈ Zion.

2   As for our harps we ˈ hung them ˈ up:
    upon the ˈ trees · that are ˈ in that ˈ land.

3   For there those who led us away captive reˈquired of us · a ˈ song:
    and those who had despoiled us demanded mirth *
        saying 'Sing us ˈ one of · the ˈ songs of ˈ Zion.'

¶ 4   How can we sing the Lord's ˈ song · in a ˈ strange ˈ land?

5   If I forget you ˈ O Jeˈrusalem:
    let my right ˈ hand forˈget its ˈ mastery.

6   Let my tongue cling to the ˈ roof of · my ˈ mouth:
    if I do not remember you * if I do not prefer Jerusalem aˈbove my ˈ chief ˈ joy.

¶ *Sung to the second half of the chant.*

138

HENRY G. LEY

1 I will give you thanks O Lord with my | whole | heart:
    even before the | gods · will I | sing your | praises.

2 I will bow down toward your holy temple * and give | thanks to · your | name:
    because of your faithfulness and your loving-kindness *
        for you have made your name and your | word su|preme · over | all things.

3 At a time when I called to you you | gave me | answer:
    and put new | strength with|in my | soul.

4 All the kings of the earth shall | praise you · O | Lord:
    for they have | heard the | words of · your | mouth;

5 And they shall sing of the | ways · of the | Lord:
    that the | glory · of the | Lord is | great.

6 For though the Lord is exalted   he looks up|on the | lowly:
    but he | humbles · the | proud · from a|far.

7 Though I walk in the midst of danger * yet will you pre|serve my | life:
    you will stretch out your hand against the fury of my enemies *
        and | your right | hand shall | save me.

8 The Lord will complete his | purpose | for me:
    your loving-kindness O Lord endures for ever *
        do not forsake the | work · of your | own | hands.

139

C. HUBERT H. PARRY

1 O Lord you have searched me | out and | known me:
    you know when I sit or when I stand *
        you comprehend my | thoughts | long be|fore.

C. HUBERT H. PARRY

2 You discern my path   and the places ˈ where I ˈ rest:
    you are acˈquainted · with ˈ all my ˈ ways.

3 For there is not a ˈ word · on my ˈ tongue:
    but you Lord ˈ know it ˈ altoˈgether.

4 You have encompassed me beˈhind · and beˈfore:
    and have ˈ laid your ˈ hand upˈon me.

† 5 Such knowledge is too ˈ wonder·ful ˈ for me:
    so ˈ high · that I ˈ cannot · enˈdure it.

6 Where shall I ˈ go · from your ˈ spirit:
    or where shall I ˈ flee ˈ from your ˈ presence?

7 If I ascend into heaven ˈ you are ˈ there:
    if I make my bed in the grave ˈ you are ˈ there ˈ also.

8 If I spread out my wings toˈwards the ˈ morning:
    or dwell in the ˈ utter·most ˈ parts · of the ˈ sea,

9 Even there your ˈ hand shall ˈ lead me:
    and ˈ your right ˈ hand shall ˈ hold me.

10 If I say   'Surely the ˈ darkness · will ˈ cover me:
    and the ˈ night ˈ will enˈclose me',

11 The darkness is no darkness with you * but the night is as ˈ clear · as the ˈ day:
    the darkness and the ˈ light are ˈ both aˈlike.

12 For you have created my ˈ inward ˈ parts:
    you knit me together ˈ in my ˈ mother's ˈ womb.

13 I will praise you for ˈ you are · to be ˈ feared:
    fearful are your ˈ acts and ˈ wonderful · your ˈ works.

14 You knew my soul * and my bones were not ˈ hidden ˈ from you:
    when I was formed in secret * and ˈ woven · in the ˈ depths · of the ˈ earth.

15 Your eyes saw my limbs when they were ˈ yet imˈperfect:
    and in your book were ˈ all my ˈ members ˈ written;

† 16 Day by ˈ day · they were ˈ fashioned:
    and not ˈ one was ˈ late in ˈ growing.

17 How deep are your thoughts to ˈ me O ˈ God:
    and how ˈ great ˈ is the ˈ sum of them!

18 Were I to count them * they are more in number ˈ than the ˈ sand:
    were I to come to the ˈ end · I would ˈ still be ˈ with you.

142

JOSEPH BARNBY

1　I call to the Lord with a ǀ loud ǀ voice:
　　with loud ǀ voice · I enǀtreat his ǀ favour.

2　I pour out my comǀplaint beǀfore him:
　　and ǀ tell him ǀ all my ǀ trouble.

3　When my spirit is faint within me you ǀ know my ǀ path:
　　in the way where I walk ǀ they have ǀ hidden · a ǀ snare for me.

4　I look to my right ǀ hand and ǀ see:
　　but ǀ no ǀ man will ǀ know me;

5　All esǀcape is ǀ gone:
　　and ǀ there is ǀ no one · who ǀ cares for me.

6　I call to you O Lord　　I say ǀ 'You are · my ǀ refuge:
　　you are my ǀ portion · in the ǀ land · of the ǀ living.'

7　Heed my loud crying　　for I am ǀ brought · very ǀ low:
　　O save me from my persecutors ǀ for they ǀ are too ǀ strong for me.

8　Bring me ǀ out of · the ǀ prison-house:
　　that ǀ I may ǀ praise your ǀ name.

†9　When you have given me ǀ my reǀward:
　　then will the ǀ righteous ǀ gather · aǀbout me.

143

C. HYLTON STEWART

1 Hear my | prayer O | Lord:
   in your faithfulness consider my petition *
      and in your | righteous·ness | give me | answer.

2 Bring not your servant | into | judgement:
   for in your sight can | no man | living · be | justified.

3 For the enemy has pursued me * he has crushed my | life · to the | ground:
   he has made me dwell in darkness like | those for | ever | dead.

4 Therefore my | spirit · grows | faint:
   and my | heart · is ap|palled with|in me.

5 I remember the days of old * I think on all that | you have | done:
   I con|sider · the | works of · your | hands.

6 I stretch out my | hands to|ward you:
   my soul yearns for you | like a | thirsty | land.

7 Be swift to hear me O Lord   for my | spirit | fails:
   hide not your face from me * lest I be like | those who · go | down · to the | Pit.

8 O let me hear of your merciful kindness in the morning * for my | trust · is in | you:
   show me the way that I should go * for | you | are my | hope.

9 Deliver me from my | enemies · O | Lord:
   for I | run to | you for | shelter.

10 Teach me to do your will   for | you are · my | God:
   let your kindly spirit | lead me · in an | even | path.

† 11 For your name's sake O Lord pre|serve my | life:
   and for the sake of your righteousness | bring me | out of | trouble.

197

145

THOMAS NORRIS

1 I will exalt you O | God my | king:
 I will bless your | name for | ever · and | ever.

2 Every | day · will I | bless you:
 and praise your | name for | ever · and | ever.

3 Great is the Lord * and wonderfully | worthy · to be | praised:
 his greatness is | past | searching | out.

4 One generation shall praise your | works · to an|other:
 and de|clare your | mighty | acts.

5 As for me * I will be talking of the glorious splendour | of your | majesty:
 I will tell the | story · of your | marvel·lous | works.

6 Men shall recount the power of your | terri·ble | deeds:
 and | I will · pro|claim your | greatness.

† 7 Their lips shall flow with the remembrance of your a|bundant | goodness:
 they shall | shout for | joy at · your | righteousness.

8 The Lord is | gracious · and com|passionate:
 slow to anger | and of | great | goodness.

9 The Lord is | loving · to | every man:
 and his mercy is | over | all his | works.

10 All creation | praises you · O | Lord:
 and your faithful | servants | bless your | name.

11 They speak of the glory | of your | kingdom:
 and | tell of · your | great | might,

† 12 That all mankind may know your | mighty | acts:
 and the glorious | splendour | of your | kingdom.

13 Your kingdom is an ever|lasting | kingdom:
 and your dominion en|dures through | all · gener|ations.

14 The Lord upholds all | those who | stumble:
 and raises up | those · that are | bowed | down.

15 The eyes of all look to | you in | hope:
 and you give them their | food in | due | season;

16 You open | wide your | hand:
and fill all things | living · with your | bounte·ous | gift.

17 The Lord is just in | all his | ways:
and | faithful · in | all his | dealings.

18 The Lord is near to all who | call up|on him:
to all who | call up|on him · in | truth.

19 He will fulfil the desire of | those that | fear him:
he will | hear their | cry and | save them.

20 The Lord preserves all | those that | love him:
but the wicked | he will | utterly · de|stroy.

† 21 My mouth shall speak the | praises · of the | Lord:
and let all flesh bless his holy | name for | ever · and | ever.

146

240

WILLIAM MARSH

1 Praise the Lord * praise the Lord | O my | soul:
while I | live · I will | praise the | Lord;

2 While I | have · any | being:
I will sing | praises | to my | God.

3 Put not your | trust in | princes:
nor in the sons of | men who | cannot | save.

4 For when their breath goes from them * they return a|gain · to the | earth:
and on that day | all their | thoughts | perish.

5 Blessèd is the man whose help is the | God of | Jacob:
whose hope is | in the | Lord his | God,

6 The God who made | heaven · and | earth:
the sea and | all | that is | in them,

† 7 Who keeps | faith for | ever:
who deals justice to | those that | are op|pressed.

8 The Lord gives | food · to the | hungry:
and | sets the | captives | free.

9 The Lord gives | sight · to the | blind:
the Lord lifts up | those · that are | bowed | down.

continued

199

WILLIAM MARSH

10 The Lord | loves the | righteous:
the Lord cares for the | stranger | in the | land.

11 He upholds the | widow · and the | fatherless:
as for the way of the wicked he | turns it | upside | down.

† 12 The Lord shall be | king for | ever:
your God O Zion shall reign through all generations * | Praise | —the | Lord.

147

CHARLES V. STANFORD

1 O praise the Lord * for it is good to sing praises | to our | God:
and to | praise him · is | joyful · and | right.

2 The Lord is re|building · Je|rusalem:
he is gathering together the | scattered | outcasts · of | Israel.

3 He heals the | broken · in | spirit:
and | binds | up their | wounds.

4 He counts the | number · of the | stars:
and | calls them | all by | name.

5 Great is our Lord and | great · is his | power:
there is no | measuring · his | under|standing.

6 The Lord re|stores the | humble:
but he brings down the | wicked | to the | dust.

7 O sing to the Lord a | song of | thanksgiving:
sing praises to our | God up|on the | harp.

8 He covers the heavens with cloud * and prepares | rain · for the | earth:
and makes the grass to | sprout up|on the | mountains.

CHARLES V. STANFORD

9　He gives the ǀ cattle · their ǀ food:
　　and feeds the young ǀ ravens · that ǀ call ǀ to him.

10　He takes no pleasure in the ǀ strength · of a ǀ horse:
　　nor does he deǀlight ǀ in any · man's ǀ legs,

† 11　But the Lord's delight is in ǀ those that ǀ fear him:
　　who ǀ wait in ǀ hope · for his ǀ mercy.

12　Praise the ǀ Lord · O Jeǀrusalem:
　　sing ǀ praises · to your ǀ God O ǀ Zion.

13　For he has strengthened the ǀ bars of · your ǀ gates:
　　and ǀ blessed your ǀ children · withǀin you.

14　He makes peace withǀin your ǀ borders:
　　and satisfies you ǀ with the ǀ finest ǀ wheat.

15　He sends his comǀmand · to the ǀ earth:
　　and his ǀ word runs ǀ very ǀ swiftly.

16　He gives ǀ snow like ǀ wool:
　　and ǀ scatters · the ǀ hoar-frost · like ǀ ashes.

17　He sprinkles his ice like ǀ morsels · of ǀ bread:
　　and the waters ǀ harden ǀ at his ǀ frost.

† 18　He sends out his ǀ word and ǀ melts them:
　　he blows with his ǀ wind · and the ǀ waters ǀ flow.

19　He made his word ǀ known to ǀ Jacob:
　　his ǀ statutes · and ǀ judgements · to ǀ Israel.

20　He has not dealt so with any ǀ other ǀ nation:
　　nor have they knowledge of his laws * ǀ Praise ǀ —the ǀ Lord.

148

CHARLES V. STANFORD

1 Praise the Lord * praise the | Lord from | heaven:
    O | praise him | in the | heights.

2 Praise him | all his | angels:
    O | praise him | all his | host.

3 Praise him | sun and | moon:
    praise him | all you | stars of | light.

4 Praise him you | highest | heaven:
    and you waters that | are a|bove the | heavens.

5 Let them praise the | name · of the | Lord:
    for he com|manded · and | they were | made.

6 He established them for | ever · and | ever:
    he made an ordinance which | shall not | pass a|way.

7 O praise the | Lord · from the | earth:
    praise him you sea-|monsters · and | all | deeps;

8 Fire and hail | mist and | snow:
    and storm-wind ful|filling | his com|mand;

9 Mountains and | all | hills:
    fruiting | trees and | all | cedars;

10 Beasts of the wild and | all | cattle:
    creeping | things and | winged | birds;

11 Kings of the earth and | all | peoples:
    princes and all | rulers | of the | world;

12 Young | men and | maidens:
    old | men and | children · to|gether.

13 Let them praise the | name · of the | Lord:
    for | his · name a|lone · is ex|alted.

14 His glory is above | earth and | heaven:
    and he has lifted | high the | horn · of his | people.

† 15 Therefore he is the praise of | all his | servants:
    of the children of Israel   a people that is near him * | Praise | —the | Lord.

149

WILLIAM CROTCH

1 O praise the Lord * and sing to the Lord a | new | song:
O praise him in the as|sembly | of the | faithful.

2 Let Israel rejoice in | him that | made him:
let the children of Zion be | joyful | in their | king.

3 Let them praise him | in the | dance:
let them sing his praise with | timbrel | and with | harp.

4 For the Lord takes de|light · in his | people :
he adorns the | meek with | his sal|vation.

† 5 Let his faithful ones ex|ult · in his | glory:
let them sing for | joy up|on their | beds.

150

244

GEORGE J. ELVEY

1 Praise the Lord * O praise | God · in his | sanctuary:
praise him in the | firma·ment | of his | power.

2 Praise him for his | mighty | acts:
praise him according to | his a|bundant | goodness.

3 Praise him in the | blast · of the | ram's horn:
praise him up|on the | lute and | harp.

4 Praise him with the | timbrel · and | dances:
praise him up|on the | strings and | pipe.

5 Praise him on the | high-·sounding | cymbals:
praise him up|on the | loud | cymbals.

6 Let everything that has breath | praise the | Lord:
O | praise | —the | Lord!

other chants overleaf

245

GEORGE S. TALBOT

1 Praise the Lord * O praise | God · in his | sanctuary:
  praise him in the | firma·ment | of his | power.

2 Praise him for his | mighty | acts:
  praise him according to | his a|bundant | goodness.

3 Praise him in the | blast · of the | ram's horn:
  praise him up|on the | lute and | harp.

4 Praise him with the | timbrel · and | dances:
  praise him up|on the | strings and | pipe.

5 Praise him on the | high-·sounding | cymbals:
  praise him up|on the | loud | cymbals.

6 Let everything that has breath | praise the | Lord:
  O | praise | —the | Lord!

246

CHARLES V. STANFORD

FULL UNISON
Praise the Lord* O praise God in his sanctua-ry; praise him in the fir - ma - ment of his power.

FULL UNISON
2. Praise him for his might - y acts: praise him according to his a - bund - ant goodness.

HARMONY
3. Praise him in the blast of the ram's horn: praise him up - on the lute and harp.